Student Make-Up Assignments

HOLT, RINEHART AND WINSTON

A Harcourt Classroom Education Company

Austin • New York • Orlando • Atlanta • San Francisco • Boston • Dallas • Toronto • London

Contributing Writers

Kathleen Ossip
Hastings-on-Hudson, NY

Jena Hiltenbrand
Austin, TX

Cover Photo Credits (tl), Tim Haske/Index Stock; (tr), Network Productions/Index Stock (b) Digital imagery® © 2003 Photodisc, Inc.

Art Credits
All art, unless otherwise noted, by Holt, Rinehart & Winston.
Page 138, Brian Stevens.

Printed in the United States of America

ISBN 0-03-065673-7

1 2 3 4 5 6 7 066 05 04 03 02 01

Contents

DIAGNOSTIC INFORMATION

STUDENT MAKE-UP ASSIGNMENTS CHECKLISTS

ALTERNATIVE QUIZZES

Chapitre 1

Chapitre 2

Chapitre 3

Chapitre 4

Chapitre 5

Chapitre 6

Chapitre 7

Chapitre 8

Chapitre 9

Chapitre 10

Chapitre 11

Chapitre 12

ANSWERS

To the Teacher

The blackline masters in this ancillary will help you keep track of the instructional material covered in a school year, so that you can give make-up information to students who missed class.

The first section of the book is a Diagnostic Table. In the first column of the table is a list of all the major presentations that make up the building blocks of the **Chapitre:** the functional expressions, the grammar, and the vocabulary. The activities listed in the other four columns are correlated to the **Grammaire supplémentaire** in the *Pupil's Edition,* the **Cahier d'activités,** the **Travaux pratiques de grammaire,** and the **Interactive CD-ROM Tutor.** This table, which gives you an overview of the presentations and opportunities for practice, can also be used as a global reference for students who need extra practice in problem areas.

The second section of the book contains the Student Make-Up Assignments Checklists. These blackline masters (one for each **étape** of the *Pupil's Edition*) can be photocopied and given to students as make-up assignments. On the left-hand side of each blackline master is a list of the presentations in each **étape.** If students missed a specific presentation (or presentations), the checklist tells them what activities they can do in the **Grammaire supplémentaire** in the *Pupil's Edition,* the **Cahier d'activités,** the **Travaux pratiques de grammaire,** or the **Interactive CD-ROM Tutor** to practice the material they missed when they were absent from class.

The third section of the book contains Alternative Quizzes that can be given to students who were absent from class when the regular Grammar and Vocabulary Quiz (Quiz A in the Testing Program) was given. The Alternative Quizzes could also be used in a different way: You can give both quizzes in the regular class, alternating rows, for example, so that students are not tempted to glance at their neighbor's paper.

The Alternative Quizzes were carefully built to reflect the same weight and level of difficulty as the regular quizzes, so that you can be assured that two students who take different versions of the quiz feel that they have been tested equally.

Diagnostic Information

The activities listed in this table are taken from the **Grammaire supplémentaire** in the *Pupil's Edition*, the **Cahier d'activités**, the **Travaux pratiques de grammaire**, and the **Interactive CD-ROM Tutor.** They provide students with extra practice in problem areas.

Grammaire = white background; **Vocabulaire** = light gray; **Comment dit-on... ?** = dark gray

CHAPITRE 1	Grammaire supplémentaire	Travaux pratiques de grammaire	Cahier d'activités	Interactive CD-ROM Tutor
Greeting people and saying goodbye			Act. 3, p. 4	Acts. 1–2, CD 1
Asking how people are and telling how you are		Act. 1, p. 1	Act. 4, p. 4	Acts. 1–2, CD 1
Asking someone's name and giving yours		Act. 5, p. 2		
Asking someone's age and giving yours	Act. 2, p. 38	Acts. 2–4, 6, pp. 1–2		Act. 3, CD 1
Expressing likes, dislikes, and preferences about things				
Negation with **ne (n')... pas**		Acts. 7–8, p. 3		
Vocabulaire: things you like and dislike		Acts. 9–11, p. 4	Act. 12, p. 8	Act. 4, CD 1
The definite articles **le, la, l'**, and **les**	Acts. 4–5, p. 39	Acts. 12–14, p. 5		
Vocabulaire: activities you like and dislike		Acts. 15–17, pp. 6–7	Acts. 18–19, p. 10	Act. 5, CD 1
Expressing likes, dislikes, and preferences about activities			Act. 16, p. 9	
Subject pronouns and **-er** verbs	Acts. 6–8, p. 40	Acts. 18–23, pp. 7–9	Acts. 14, 17, pp. 9–10	Act. 6, CD 1
CHAPITRE 2	**Grammaire supplémentaire**	**Travaux pratiques de grammaire**	**Cahier d'activités**	**Interactive CD-ROM Tutor**
Vocabulaire: school subjects		Acts. 1–4, pp.10–11	Acts. 2–5, 7, pp. 14–16	Act. 1, CD 1
Agreeing and disagreeing			Act. 6, p. 15	
si versus **oui**	Acts. 1–2, p. 66	Act. 5, p. 11	Act. 8, p. 16	
Asking for and giving information	Act. 3, p. 66			
Vocabulaire: times of the day		Act. 6, p. 12		
The verb **avoir**	Acts. 3–6, pp. 66–68	Acts. 7–9, pp. 12–13	Act. 12, p. 17	Act. 2, CD 1
Vocabulaire: days of the week		Acts. 10–12, pp. 13–14	Acts. 14–15, pp. 18–19	Act. 3, CD 1
Vocabulaire: numbers 21–59		Acts. 13–14, pp. 14–15	Act. 11, p. 17	
Telling when you have class		Acts. 15–17, p. 15	Act. 13, p. 18	Act. 4, CD 1
Asking for and expressing opinions	Acts. 7–9, p. 69	Acts. 18–20, p. 16	Acts. 17–19, pp. 20–21	Acts. 5–6, CD 1

CHAPITRE 3	Grammaire supplémentaire	Travaux pratiques de grammaire	Cahier d'activités	Interactive CD-ROM Tutor
Vocabulaire: school supplies		Acts. 1–3, pp. 17–18	Acts. 2–3, p. 26	Act. 1, CD 1
Making and responding to requests			Act. 4b, p. 27	
The indefinite articles **un, une**, and **des**	Acts. 1–3, p. 94	Acts. 4–7, pp. 18–19		Act. 2, CD 1
Asking others what they need and telling what you need	Act. 3, p. 94		Acts. 5–6, p. 28	
Vocabulaire: for school and fun		Acts. 8–9, p. 20		Act. 3, CD 1
Telling what you'd like and what you'd like to do				
The demonstrative adjectives **ce,cet, cette**, and **ces**	Acts. 5–6, pp. 95–96	Acts. 10–11, p. 21	Acts. 7–8, p. 29	
Vocabulaire: colors		Act. 12, p. 22	Acts. 9–10, pp. 29–30	
Adjective agreement and placement	Acts. 7–8, p. 96	Acts. 13–15, pp. 22–23	Acts. 11–12, p. 30	Acts. 4–5, CD 1
Vocabulaire: numbers 60–201		Acts. 16–18, p. 24	Acts. 15–16, p. 32	Act. 6, CD 1
Getting someone's attention; asking for information; expressing thanks			Acts. 18–19, p. 34	
CHAPITRE 4	**Grammaire supplémentaire**	**Travaux pratiques de grammaire**	**Cahier d'activités**	**Interactive CD-ROM Tutor**
Vocabulaire: sports and hobbies		Acts. 1–2, p. 25	Act. 4, p. 38	Act. 1, CD 1
Expressions with **faire** and **jouer**	Acts. 1–3, pp. 128–129	Acts. 3–4, p. 26	Act. 3, p. 38	Act. 2, CD 1
Telling how much you like or dislike something			Act. 5, p. 39	
Question formation	Act. 3, p. 129	Acts. 5–6, p. 27	Act. 8, p. 40	
Exchanging information	Acts. 4–5, p. 129			
The partitive and negative sentences	Act. 4, p. 129	Acts. 7–8, p. 28	Act. 10, p. 41	
The verb **faire**	Acts. 5–6, pp. 129–130	Acts. 9–10, p. 29	Act. 11, p. 41	Act. 3, CD 1
The pronoun **on**	Act. 7, p. 130	Act. 11, p. 30	Act. 9, p. 41	
Vocabulaire: weather		Act. 12, p. 30		
Vocabulaire: months of the year		Acts. 13–14, p. 31	Act. 17, p. 44	
Vocabulaire: seasons		Act. 16, p. 32	Acts. 12–14, p. 42	Act. 4, CD 1
Making, accepting, and turning down suggestions			Act. 19, p. 45	Act. 5, CD 1
Adverbs of frequency	Acts. 9–10, p. 131	Acts. 18–20, p. 34	Acts. 20–22, pp. 45–46	Act. 6, CD 1

CHAPITRE 5	Grammaire supplémentaire	Travaux pratiques de grammaire	Cahier d'activités	Interactive CD-ROM Tutor
Making suggestions; making excuses;			Acts. 7–8, pp. 51–52	
Vocabulaire: foods and beverages		Acts. 1–4, pp. 35–36	Act. 3, p. 50	Acts. 1–2, CD 2
Making a recommendation		Act. 5, p. 36		
The verb **prendre**	Acts. 1–2, p. 160	Acts. 6–7, p. 37	Act. 5, p. 51	Act. 3, CD 2
Getting someone's attention; ordering food and beverages			Acts. 10–12, p. 53	
The imperative	Acts. 3–6, pp. 161–162	Acts. 8–10, p. 38	Acts. 13, 15, p. 54	Act. 4, CD 2
Inquiring about and expressing likes and dislikes		Acts. 11–12, p. 39	Acts. 19–21, pp. 56–57	
Paying the check	Act. 7, p. 163	Acts. 13–14, pp. 39–40	Acts. 23–24, pp. 57–58	Acts. 5–6, CD 2
CHAPITRE 6	**Grammaire supplémentaire**	**Travaux pratiques de grammaire**	**Cahier d'activités**	**Interactive CD-ROM Tutor**
Making plans				
Vocabulaire: things to do			Acts. 1–2, p. 61	
Le with days of the week	Acts. 1–2, p. 190	Acts. 3–4, p. 42		
The verb **aller**	Acts. 3–4, p. 191	Acts. 5–6, p. 43	Act. 7, p. 63	Act. 1, CD 2
Vocabulaire: places to go		Acts. 7–9, pp. 44–45	Acts. 6, 8, pp. 63–64	Acts. 2–3, CD 2
Contractions with **à**	Acts. 5–6, pp. 191–192	Acts. 10–11, p. 45		
Extending and responding to invitations			Acts. 11–14, pp. 65–66	Act. 4, CD 2
The verb **vouloir**	Acts. 7–8, p. 192	Acts. 12–13, p. 46	Acts. 15–16, pp. 66–67	Act. 5, CD 2
Arranging to meet someone		Acts. 14–17, pp. 47–48	Acts. 19–20, pp. 68–69	Act. 6, CD 2
Information questions	Acts. 9–10, p. 193	Acts. 18–21, pp. 49–50	Acts. 21–22, p. 69	

CHAPITRE 7	Grammaire supplémentaire	Travaux pratiques de grammaire	Cahier d'activités	Interactive CD-ROM Tutor
Identifying people				
Vocabulaire: family members		Acts. 1–2, p. 51	Acts. 2a, 4, pp. 74–75	Act. 1, CD 2
Possession with **de**		Acts. 3–4, p. 52	Acts. 2b, 7b, pp. 74–76	
Possessive adjectives	Acts. 2–4, pp. 218–219	Acts. 5–7, p. 53	Acts. 6–7a, pp. 75–76	
Introducing people			Act. 8, p. 76	
Vocabulaire: adjectives to describe people		Acts. 8–9, p. 54	Acts. 9–10, p. 77	Act. 3, CD 2
Describing and characterizing people			Act. 13, p. 78	
Adjective agreement	Acts. 5–8, pp. 219–220	Acts. 10–14, pp. 55–57	Acts. 11–12, pp. 77–78	Act. 2, CD 2
The verb **être**		Acts. 15–17, pp. 57–58	Acts. 14–15, pp. 78–79	Act. 4, CD 2
Asking for, giving, and refusing permission	Act. 10, p. 221		Act. 21, p. 81	Act. 5, CD 2
Vocabulaire: chores	Act. 11, p. 221	Acts. 18–21, pp. 59–60	Acts. 17–18, 20, 22–23, pp. 80–82	Act. 6, CD 2

CHAPITRE 8	Grammaire supplémentaire	Travaux pratiques de grammaire	Cahier d'activités	Interactive CD-ROM Tutor
Vocabulaire: foods		Acts. 1–4, pp. 61–62	Acts. 3–5, pp. 86–87	Acts. 1–2, CD 2
The partitive and indefinite articles	Acts. 1–3, p. 252	Acts. 5–9, pp. 63–65	Act. 6, p. 87	Act. 3, CD 2
Expressing need			Act. 8, p. 88	
avoir besoin de	Act. 4, p. 253	Act. 10, p. 65	Act. 9, p. 88	
Making, accepting, and declining requests; telling someone what to do			Acts. 10–12, p. 89	
The verb **pouvoir**	Acts. 5–6, p. 253	Acts. 11–12, p. 66	Acts. 13–14, p. 90	Act. 4, CD 2
Vocabulaire: expressions of quantity		Act. 13, p. 67	Acts. 15–17, pp. 90–91	Act. 5, CD 2
de with expressions of quantity	Act. 8, p. 254	Acts. 14–16, pp. 67–68		
Vocabulaire: meals		Acts. 17–18, p. 69	Acts. 19–20, p. 92	
Offering, accepting, or refusing food			Acts. 21–22, pp. 92–93	Act. 6, CD 2
The pronoun **en**	Acts. 9–11, pp. 254–255	Acts. 19–20, p. 70	Act. 23, p. 93	

CHAPITRE 9	Grammaire supplémentaire	Travaux pratiques de grammaire	Cahier d'activités	Interactive CD-ROM Tutor
Asking for and expressing opinions			Act. 2, p. 98	
Inquiring about and relating past events			Act. 3, p. 98	
The **passé composé** with **avoir**	Acts. 1–3, pp. 284–285	Acts. 1–7, pp. 71–74	Acts. 4, 6–7, pp. 98–99	Act. 1, CD 3
Placement of adverbs with the **passé composé**	Acts. 4–5, p. 285	Act. 8, p. 74		
Vocabulaire: daily events		Acts. 9–10, p. 75		Acts. 2–3, CD 3
Making and answering a phone call		Acts. 11–12, p. 76	Acts. 13–14, p. 102	Acts. 4–5, CD 3
-**re** verbs: **répondre**	Acts. 6–8, p. 286	Acts. 13–14, p. 77	Acts. 15–16, p. 103	
Sharing confidences and consoling others; asking for and giving advice			Acts. 18–22, pp. 104–105	Act. 6, CD 3
The object pronouns **le, la, lui,** and **leur**	Acts. 9–10, p. 287	Acts. 15–16, p. 78		
CHAPITRE 10	**Grammaire supplémentaire**	**Travaux pratiques de grammaire**	**Cahier d'activités**	**Interactive CD-ROM Tutor**
Vocabulaire: clothing		Acts. 1–3, pp. 79–80	Acts. 2–4, p. 110	Acts. 1–2, CD 3
The verbs **mettre** and **porter**	Acts. 1–3, p. 314	Acts. 4–6, pp. 80–81	Acts. 6–7, p. 111	
Asking for and giving advice			Acts. 8–9, p. 112	
Expressing need; Inquiring		Act. 7, p. 82	Acts. 10–11, p. 113	
Grammaire: adjectives used as nouns	Act. 4, p. 315	Act. 8, p. 82	Act. 12, p. 114	
-**ir** verbs: **choisir**	Acts. 5–7, pp. 315–316	Acts. 9–12, pp. 83–84	Acts. 14–16, p. 115	Act. 3, CD 3
Aking for an opinion, paying a compliment		Acts. 13–15, pp. 85–86	Acts. 17–19, pp. 116–117	Act. 5, CD 3
The direct object pronouns **le, la,** and **les**	Acts. 8–9, pp. 316–317	Acts. 16–17, pp. 86–87	Act. 21, p. 117	Act. 4, CD 3
Hesitating; making a decision			Act. 22, p. 118	
il/elle est... versus. **c'est...**	Act. 10, p. 317	Act. 18, p. 87	Act. 23, p. 118	Act. 6, CD 3

CHAPITRE 11	Grammaire supplémentaire	Travaux pratiques de grammaire	Cahier d'activités	Interactive CD-ROM Tutor
Vocabulaire: vacation places and activities		Acts. 1–4, pp. 88–89	Act. 2, p. 122	Act. 1, CD 3
Inquiring about and sharing future plans; expressing indecision; expressing wishes			Act. 6, p. 123	
The preposition **à** and **en**	Act. 3, p. 342	Act. 7, p. 91		
Vocabulaire: travel items		Acts. 8–9, p. 92	Acts. 10–11, p. 125	Act. 2, CD 3
Reminding; reassuring			Act. 13, p. 126	
The verbs **partir**, **sortir** and **dormir**	Acts. 6–8, p. 344	Acts. 11–12, pp. 93–94	Act. 12, p. 125	Act. 3, CD 3
Seeing someone off			Acts. 14–16, p. 127	
Asking for and expressing opinions			Acts. 17–19, pp. 128–129	Act. 4, CD 3
CHAPITRE 12	**Grammaire supplémentaire**	**Travaux pratiques de grammaire**	**Cahier d'activités**	**Interactive CD-ROM Tutor**
Vocabulaire: things to do and buy in town		Acts. 1–4, pp. 98–99	Acts. 2–5, pp. 134–135	Acts. 1–2, CD 3
Pointing out places and things			Act. 8, p. 136	
Making and responding to requests			Acts. 9–11, p. 137	
Asking for advice and making suggestions				
Vocabulaire: means of transportation		Acts. 11–15, pp. 103–104	Acts. 12–14, p. 138	Act. 4, CD 3
The pronoun **y**	Acts. 6–8, p. 378	Acts. 16–17, p. 105	Acts. 15–16, p. 139	Act. 5, CD 3
Vocabulaire: locations		Acts. 19–21, pp. 106–107	Acts. 18–20, p. 140	
Contractions with **de**	Acts. 9–10, p. 379	Act. 18, p. 106	Act. 21, p. 141	
Asking for and giving directions			Acts. 22–24, pp. 141–142	Act. 6, CD 3

Student Make-Up Assignments Checklist

Nom______________ Classe__________ Date__________

Chapitre Préliminaire

CHAPITRE PRELIMINAIRE Student Make-Up Checklist

Pupil's Edition, pp. xxvi–11

The material on pages xxvi–11 can best be learned and practiced in conjunction with Audio CD 1 in the Audio Program.

Study the maps of Europe, Africa, French Polynesia, and America on pp. xxvi–1.	☐ Make a list of the countries where French is spoken on these different continents.
Read the information on pp. 2–3.	☐ Make a list of other native French speakers of whom you are aware, along with some of their accomplishments.
Read the information on p. 5.	☐ Do Activity 1, p. 5. Write an introduction for yourself in French. Then, write a dialogue where you ask some students their names and they respond.
Study **l'alphabet** on p. 6.	☐ Do Activity 2, p. 7 as a writing activity.
Study the accents on p. 8.	☐ Find in your French-English glossary in the back of your book, five more words for each different accent.
Study the French numbers from 0 through 20 on p. 9.	☐ Do Activity 6, p. 9 as a writing activity. ☐ Practice pronouncing the French numbers out loud.
Study the picture of common classroom items on p. 10.	☐ Match the name of each student with a command from the box.
Read the study tips on p. 11.	☐ List all the suggestions that you plan to follow during your first year of French study.

CHAPITRE 1

Nom________________ Classe__________ Date__________

Faisons connaissance!

PREMIERE ETAPE Student Make-Up Assignments Checklist

Pupil's Edition, pp. 22–25

Study the expressions in the **Comment dit-on... ?** box on page 22: greeting people and saying goodbye. You should know how to greet someone and how to say goodbye to someone.	☐ Do Activity 8, p. 22 as a writing activity. ☐ For additional practice, do Activity 3, p. 4 in the **Cahier d'activités.** ☐ For additional practice, do Activities 1–2, CD 1 in the **Interactive CD-ROM Tutor.**
Study the expressions in the **Comment dit-on... ?** box on page 23: asking how people are and telling how you are. You should know how to ask how your friend is and say how you are.	☐ Do Activity 10, p. 24. Do the first part only. ☐ Do Activity 11, p. 24 as a writing activity. ☐ For additional practice, do Activity 4, p. 4 in the **Cahier d'activités.** ☐ For additional practice, do Activity 1, p. 1 in the **Travaux pratiques de grammaire.** ☐ For additional practice, do Activities 1–2, CD 1 in the **Interactive CD-ROM Tutor.**
Study the expressions in the **Comment dit-on... ?** box on page 24: asking someone's name and giving yours. You should know how to ask someone his or her name and give your name.	☐ Do Activity 14, p. 25 as a writing activity. Write a conversation in which you introduce yourself to a classmate. ☐ For additional practice, do Activity 2, p. 38 in the **Grammaire supplémentaire.** ☐ For additional practice, do Activity 5, p. 2 in the **Travaux pratiques de grammaire.**
Study the expressions in the **Comment dit-on... ?** box on page 25: asking someone's age and giving yours. You should know how to find out someone's age and give your age.	☐ Do Activity 16, p. 25 as a writing activity. Write a conversation between three classmates in which they introduce each other. ☐ Do Activity 17, p. 25. ☐ For additional practice, do Activity 2, p. 38 in the **Grammaire supplémentaire.** ☐ For additional practice, do Activities 2–4, 6, pp. 1–2 in the **Travaux pratiques de grammaire.** ☐ For additional practice, do Activity 3, CD 1 in the **Interactive CD-ROM Tutor.**

Nom ______________________ Classe ______________ Date ______________

CHAPITRE 1

PREMIERE ETAPE Self-Test

Can you greet people and say goodbye?	How would you say hello and goodbye to the following people? 1. a classmate 2. your French teacher
Can you ask how people are and tell how you are?	Can you ask how someone is? If someone asks you how you are, what do you say if . . . 1. you feel great? 2. you feel OK? 3. you don't feel well?
Can you ask someone's name and age and give yours?	How would you . . . 1. ask someone's name? 2. tell someone your name? How would you . . . 1. find out someone's age? 2. tell someone how old you are?

For an online self-test, go to **go.hrw.com**.

WA3 POITIERS-1

Nom ________________ Classe ____________ Date ____________

Faisons connaissance!

DEUXIEME ETAPE Student Make-Up Assignments Checklist

Pupil's Edition, pp. 26–29

Study the expressions in the **Comment dit-on... ?** box on page 26: expressing likes, dislikes, and preferences about things. You should know how to ask if someone likes or dislikes something and say what you like and dislike.	☐ For additional practice, do Activities 3–5, p. 39 in the **Grammaire supplémentaire.**
Study the grammar presentation in the **Note de grammaire** box on page 26: negation.	☐ Do Activity 19, p. 26 as a writing activity. ☐ For additional practice, do Activities 7–8, p. 3 in the **Travaux pratiques de grammaire.**
Study the **Vocabulaire** on page 27.	☐ For additional practice, do Activity 12, p. 8 in the **Cahier d'activités.** ☐ For additional practice, do Activities 9–11, p. 4 in the **Travaux pratiques de grammaire.** ☐ For additional practice, do Activity 4, CD 1 in the **Interactive CD-ROM Tutor.**
Study the grammar presentation in the **Grammaire** box on page 28: the definite articles **le, la l'**, and **les.**	☐ Do Activity 21, p. 29 as a writing activity. ☐ Do Activity 22, p. 29. ☐ Do Activity 23, p. 29. ☐ For additional practice, do Activities 4–5, p. 39 in the **Grammaire supplémentaire.** ☐ For additional practice, do Activities 12–14, p. 5 in the **Travaux pratiques de grammaire.**

DEUXIEME ETAPE Self-Test

Can you express likes, dislikes, and preferences about things?

Can you tell what you like and dislike, using the verb **aimer**?

1. ice cream
2. soccer
3. vacation
4. chocolate
5. the movies

For an online self-test, go to **go.hrw.com**.

WA3 POITIERS-1

Nom _______________ Classe _______________ Date _______________

Faisons connaissance!

TROISIEME ETAPE Student Make-Up Assignments Checklist

Pupil's Edition, pp. 31–35

Study the **Vocabulaire** on page 31.	☐ For additional practice, do Activities 18–19, p. 10 in the **Cahier d'activités.** ☐ For additional practice, do Activities 15–17, pp. 6–7 in the **Travaux pratiques de grammaire.** ☐ For additional practice, do Activity 5, CD 1 in the **Interactive CD-ROM Tutor.**
Study the expressions in the **Comment dit-on... ?** box on page 32: expressing likes, dislikes, and preferences about activities. You should know how to ask if someone likes an activity, say what you like and don't like to do, and say what you prefer to do.	☐ Do Part a of Activity 25, p. 32 as a writing activity. ☐ For additional practice, do Activity 16, p. 9 in the **Cahier d'activités.**
Study the grammar presentation in the **Grammaire** box on page 33: subject pronouns and **-er** verbs.	☐ Do Activity 26, p. 33 as a writing activity. ☐ Do Activity 27, p. 34 as a writing activity. ☐ Do Part a of Activity 28, p. 34. ☐ Do Activity 30, p. 35. ☐ For additional practice, do Activities 6–8, p. 40 in the **Grammaire supplémentaire.** ☐ For additional practice, do Activities 14 and 17, pp. 9–10 in the **Cahier d'activités.** ☐ For additional practice, do Activities 18–23, pp. 7–9 in the **Travaux pratiques de grammaire.** ☐ For additional practice, do Activity 6, CD 1 in the **Interactive CD-ROM Tutor.**

Nom ______________________ Classe ______________ Date ______________

CHAPITRE 1

TROISIEME ETAPE Self-Test

Can you express likes, dislikes, and preferences about activities?

Can you tell in French what these people like, dislike, or prefer?

1. Robert never studies.
2. Emilie thinks reading is the greatest.
3. Hervé prefers going shopping.
4. Nathalie never watches TV.
5. Nicole is always sleeping.

For an online self-test, go to **go.hrw.com**.

WA3 POITIERS-1

CHAPITRE 2

Nom______________ Classe__________ Date__________

Vive l'école!

PREMIERE ETAPE Student Make-Up Assignments Checklist

Pupil's Edition, pp. 51–54

Study the **Vocabulaire** on page 51.	☐ Do Activity 9, p. 52 as a writing activity. ☐ Do Activity 10, p. 53. ☐ For additional practice, do Activities 2–5 and 7, pp. 14–16 in the **Cahier d'activités.** ☐ For additional practice, do Activities 1–4, pp. 10–11 in the **Travaux pratiques de grammaire.** ☐ For additional practice, do Activity 1, CD 1 in the **Interactive CD-ROM Tutor.**
Study the expressions in the **Comment dit-on... ?** box on page 54: agreeing and disagreeing. You should know how to agree and disagree.	☐ For additional practice, do Activity 6, p. 15 in the **Cahier d'activités.**
Study the grammar presentation in the **Note de grammaire** on page 54: negation.	☐ Do Activity 12, p. 54 as a writing activity. Write a conversation based on the clues from the activity. ☐ Do Activity 13, p. 54 as a writing activity. Write a conversation based on the clues from the activity. ☐ For additional practice, do Activities 1–2, p. 66 in the **Grammaire supplémentaire.** ☐ For additional practice, do Activity 8, p. 16 in the **Cahier d'activités.** ☐ For additional practice, do Activity 5, p. 11 in the **Travaux pratiques de grammaire.**

Nom ______________________ Classe ______________ Date ______________

PREMIERE ETAPE Self-Test

Can you agree and disagree?	How would you agree if your friend said the following? How would you disagree with your friend? 1. J'adore l'histoire! 2. J'aime les sciences nat. Et toi? 3. Je n'aime pas le français.

For an online self-test, go to **go.hrw.com**.

WA3 POITIERS-2

CHAPITRE 2

CHAPITRE 2

Nom______________________ Classe______________ Date______________

Vive l'école!

DEUXIEME ETAPE Student Make-Up Assignments Checklist

Pupil's Edition, pp. 55–59

Study the expressions in the **Comment dit-on... ?** box on page 55: asking for and giving information. You should know how to ask about someone's classes and how to tell about yours.	☐ For additional practice, do Activity 3, p. 66 in the **Grammaire supplémentaire.**
Study the **Vocabulaire** on page 55.	☐ Do Activity 14, p. 55 as a writing activity. ☐ For additional practice, do Activity 6, p. 12 in the **Travaux pratiques de grammaire.**
Study the grammar presentation in the **Grammaire** box on page 55: the verb **avoir.**	☐ Do Activity 15, p. 56 as a writing activity. ☐ For additional practice, do Activities 3–6, pp. 66–68 in the **Grammaire supplémentaire.** ☐ For additional practice, do Activity 12, p. 17 in the **Cahier d'activités.** ☐ For additional practice, do Activities 7–9, pp. 12–13 in the **Travaux pratiques de grammaire.** ☐ For additional practice, do Activity 2, CD 1 in the **Interactive CD-ROM Tutor.**
Study the **Vocabulaire** on page 56.	☐ Do Activity 16, p. 57 as a writing activity. ☐ Do Activity 17, p. 57. ☐ For additional practice, do Activities 14–15, pp. 18–19 in the **Cahier d'activités.** ☐ For additional practice, do Activities 10–12, pp. 13–14 in the **Travaux pratiques de grammaire.** ☐ For additional practice, do Activity 3, CD 1 in the **Interactive CD-ROM Tutor.**
Study the **Vocabulaire** on page 57.	☐ Do Activity 19, p. 58 as a writing activity. Write the numbers out. ☐ For additional practice, do Activity 11, p. 17 in the **Cahier d'activités.** ☐ For additional practice, do Activities 13–14, pp. 14–15 in the **Travaux pratiques de grammaire.**

Study the expressions in the **Comment dit-on... ?** box on page 58: telling when you have class. You should know how to ask when you have a certain class.	☐ Do Activity 21, p. 59 as a writing activity. ☐ Do the first part of Activity 22, p. 59 by filling out a blank schedule with the time your classes meet. ☐ Do Activity 23, p. 59. ☐ For additional practice, do Activity 13, p. 18 in the **Cahier d'activités.** ☐ For additional practice, do Activities 15–17, p. 15 in the **Travaux pratiques de grammaire.** ☐ For additional practice, do Activity 4, CD 1 in the **Interactive CD-ROM Tutor.**

DEUXIEME ETAPE Self-Test

Can you ask for and give information?	How would you ask . . . 1. what subjects your friend has in the morning? 2. what subjects your friend has in the afternoon? 3. what subjects your friend has on Tuesdays? 4. if your friend has music class? 5. if your friend has English today? How would you say in French that the following students have these classes, using the verb **avoir?** 1. you / French and choir 2. Paul / physics 3. we / gym 4. Francine and Séverine / Spanish
Can you tell when you have class?	How would you ask your friend at what time he or she has the classes represented by the drawings in Activity 4 on the **Que sais-je?** page 72? How would you tell your friend that you have the following classes at the times given? Look at the drawings in Activity 5 on the **Que sais-je?** page 72?

For an online self-test, go to **go.hrw.com**.

WA3 POITIERS-2

Nom _______________ Classe _______________ Date _______________

Vive l'école!

TROISIEME ETAPE Student Make-Up Assignments Checklist

Pupil's Edition, pp. 61–63

Study the expressions in the **Comment dit-on... ?** box on page 61: asking for and expressing opinions. You should know how to ask someone's opinion, how to express a favorable and an unfavorable opinion and indifference.

- ☐ Do Activity 25, p. 62 as a writing activity.
- ☐ Do Activity 26, p. 62.
- ☐ Do Activity 27, p. 62 as a writing activity. Write a conversation based on the clues from the activity.
- ☐ Do Activity 28, p. 63. Write a conversation based on the clues from the activity.
- ☐ For additional practice, do Activities 7–9, p. 69 in the **Grammaire supplémentaire.**
- ☐ For additional practice, do Activities 17–19, pp. 20–21 in the **Cahier d'activités.**
- ☐ For additional practice, do Activities 18–20, p. 16 in the **Travaux pratiques de grammaire.**
- ☐ For additional practice, do Activities 5–6, CD 1 in the **Interactive CD-ROM Tutor.**

TROISIEME ETAPE Self-Test

Can you ask for and express opinions?	How would you tell your friend that your geography class is . . . 1. fascinating? 2. not so great? 3. boring?

For an online self-test, go to **go.hrw.com**.

WA3 POITIERS-2

CHAPITRE 3

Nom_______________ Classe__________ Date__________

Tout pour la rentrée

PREMIERE ETAPE Student Make-Up Assignments Checklist

Pupil's Edition, pp. 79–82

Study the **Vocabulaire** on page 79.	☐ Do Activity 7, p. 80. ☐ For additional practice, do Activities 2–3, p. 26 in the **Cahier d'activités.** ☐ For additional practice, do Activities 1–3, pp. 17–18 in the **Travaux pratiques de grammaire.** ☐ For additional practice, do Activity 1, CD 1 in the **Interactive CD-ROM Tutor.**
Study the expressions in the **Comment dit-on... ?** box on page 80: making and responding to requests. You should know how to ask someone for something and how to give something to someone.	☐ For additional practice, do Activity 4b, p. 27 in the **Cahier d'activités.**
Study the grammar presentation in the **Grammaire** box on page 81: the indefinite articles **un, une,** and **des.**	☐ Do Activity 10, p. 81 ☐ For additional practice, do Activities 1–3, p. 94 in the **Grammaire supplémentaire.** ☐ For additional practice, do Activities 4–7, pp. 18–19 in the **Travaux pratiques de grammaire.** ☐ For additional practice, do Activity 2, CD 1 in the **Interactive CD-ROM Tutor.**
Study the expressions in the **Comment dit-on... ?** box on page 82: asking others what they need and telling what you need. You should know how to ask what someone needs and say what you need.	☐ Do Activity 11, p. 82. Write about your classes and what you need. ☐ Do Activity 12, p. 82. ☐ Do Activity 13, p. 82 as a writing activity. Write a conversation in which you ask a classmate for school supplies. ☐ For additional practice, do Activity 3, p. 94 in the **Grammaire supplémentaire.** ☐ For additional practice, do Activities 5–6, p. 28 in the **Cahier d'activités.**

Nom________________ Classe__________ Date__________

PREMIERE ETAPE Self-Test

Can you make and respond to requests?	How would you ask for the following items using the verb **avoir?** How would you respond to someone's request for one of the items in the pictures for Activity 1 on the **Que sais-je?** page 100?
Can you ask others what they need?	How would you ask your friend what he or she needs for each of these school subjects? Look at the drawings for Activity 2 on the **Que sais-je?** page 100.
Can you tell what you need?	How would you tell your friend that you need . . . 1. a calculator and an eraser for math? 2. a binder and some sheets of paper for Spanish class? 3. some pens and a notebook for English? 4. a pencil and a ruler for geometry? 5. a backpack and a book for history?

For an online self-test, go to go.hrw.com.

WA3 POITIERS-3

CHAPITRE 3

Nom______________________ Classe____________ Date____________

Tout pour la rentrée

DEUXIEME ETAPE Student Make-Up Assignments Checklist

Pupil's Edition, pp. 84–87

Study the **Vocabulaire** on page 84.	☐ For additional practice, do Activities 8–9, p. 20 in the **Travaux pratiques de grammaire.** ☐ For additional practice, do Activity 3, CD 1 in the **Interactive CD-ROM Tutor.**
Study the expressions in the **Comment dit-on... ?** box on page 85: telling what you'd like and what you'd like to do. You should know how to say what you'd like and what you'd like to do.	☐ Do Activity 16, p. 85 as a writing activity. Write a conversation between three friends discussing what they want to do. ☐ Do Activity 17, p. 85. ☐ Do Activity 18, p. 85.
Study the grammar presentation in the **Grammaire** box on page 85: the demonstrative adjectives **ce, cet, cette,** and **ces.**	☐ Do Activity 19, p. 86 as a writing activity. Rewrite the sentences using the correct demostrative adjective. ☐ Do Activity 20, p. 86 as a writing activity. Write small conversations between two people discussing the items in the pictures. ☐ For additional practice, do Activities 5–6, pp. 95–96 in the **Grammaire supplémentaire.** ☐ For additional practice, do Activities 7–8, p. 29 in the **Cahier d'activités.** ☐ For additional practice, do Activities 10–11, p. 21 in the **Travaux pratiques de grammaire.**
Study the **Vocabulaire** on page 86.	☐ Do Activity 21, p. 87 as a writing activity. ☐ For additional practice, do Activities 9–10, pp. 29–30 in the **Cahier d'activités.** ☐ For additional practice, do Activity 12, p. 22 in the **Travaux pratiques de grammaire.**

Study the grammar presentation in the **Grammaire** box on page 87: adjective agreement and placement.

- ☐ Do Activity 22, p. 87.
- ☐ For additional practice, do Activities 7–8 p. 96 in the **Grammaire supplémentaire.**
- ☐ For additional practice, do Activities 11–12, p. 30 in the **Cahier d'activités.**
- ☐ For additional practice, do Activities 13–15, pp. 22–23 in the **Travaux pratiques de grammaire.**
- ☐ For additional practice, do Activities 4–5, CD 1 in the **Interactive CD-ROM Tutor.**

DEUXIEME ETAPE Self-Test

Can you tell what you'd like and what you'd like to do?

How would you tell your friend that you'd like . . .

1. those white sneakers?
2. this blue bag?
3. that purple and black pencil case?
4. to listen to music and talk on the phone?
5. to go shopping?

For an online self-test, go to go.hrw.com.

WA3 POITIERS-3

Nom ____________ Classe ____________ Date ____________

Tout pour la rentrée

TROISIEME ETAPE Student Make-Up Assignments Checklist

Pupil's Edition, pp. 88–91

Study the **Vocabulaire** on page 88.	☐ Do Activity 24, p. 89. ☐ Do Activity 25, p. 89 as a writing activity. ☐ Do Activity 26, p. 90. ☐ For additional practice, do Activities 15–16, p. 32 in the **Cahier d'activités.** ☐ For additional practice, do Activities 16–18, p. 24 in the **Travaux pratiques de grammaire.** ☐ For additional practice, do Activity 6, CD 1 in the **Interactive CD-ROM Tutor.**
Study the expressions in the **Comment dit-on... ?** box on page 90: getting someone's attention; asking for information; expressing and responding to thanks. You should know how to get someone's attention, how to ask how much something costs, and express thanks.	☐ Do Activity 28, p. 90 as a writing activity. Write a conversation between a customer and a salesperson. ☐ Do Activity 29, p. 91 as a writing activity. Write a conversation between a customer and a salesperson. ☐ For additional practice, do Activities 18–19, p. 34 in the **Cahier d'activités.**

Nom ______________________ Classe ______________ Date ______________

TROISIEME ETAPE Self-Test

Can you get someone's attention, ask for information, express and respond to thanks?	What would you say in a store to . . . 1. get a salesperson's attention? 2. politely ask the price of something? 3. thank a clerk for helping you?

For an online self-test, go to **go.hrw.com**.

WA3 POITIERS-3

CHAPITRE 3

CHAPITRE 4

Nom ________________ Classe ____________ Date ____________

Sports et passe-temps

PREMIERE ETAPE Student Make-Up Assignments Checklist

Pupil's Edition, pp. 112–115

Study the **Vocabulaire** on page 112.	☐ For additional practice, do Activity 4, p. 38 in the **Cahier d'activités**. ☐ For additional practice, do Activities 1–2, p. 25 in the **Travaux pratiques de grammaire.** ☐ For additional practice, do Activity 1, CD 1 in the **Interactive CD-ROM Tutor.**
Study the grammar presentation in the **Grammaire** box on page 113: expressions with **faire** and **jouer.**	☐ Do Activity 7, p. 113. ☐ Do Activity 8, p. 113 as a writing activity. ☐ For additional practice, do Activities 1–3, pp. 128–129 in the **Grammaire supplémentaire.** ☐ For additional practice, do Activity 3, p. 38 in the **Cahier d'activités.** ☐ For additional practice, do Activities 3–4, p. 26 in the **Travaux pratiques de grammaire.** ☐ For additional practice, do Activity 2, CD 1 in the **Interactive CD-ROM Tutor.**
Study the expressions in the **Comment dit-on... ?** box on page 114: telling how much you like or dislike something. You should know how to tell how much you like or dislike something.	☐ Do Activity 10, p. 114 as a writing activity. ☐ Do Activity 11, p. 115 as a writing activity. ☐ For additional practice, do Activity 5, p. 39 in the **Cahier d'activités.**

Study the grammar presentation in the **Grammaire** box on page 115: question formation.

- ☐ Do Activity 12, p. 115 as a writing activity. Write a conversation between you and a friend in which you discuss sports and hobbies.
- ☐ For additional practice, do Activity 3, p. 129 in the **Grammaire supplémentaire.**
- ☐ For additional practice, do Activity 8, p. 40 in the **Cahier d'activités.**
- ☐ For additional practice, do Activities 5–6, p. 27 in the **Travaux pratiques de grammaire.**

PREMIERE ETAPE Self-Test

Can you tell how much you like or dislike something?

Can you tell someone how much you like or dislike the activities in the drawings in Activity 1 on the **Que sais-je?** page 134?

Can you tell someone which sports and activities you enjoy a lot? Which ones you don't enjoy at all?

For an online self-test, go to go.hrw.com.

WA3 QUEBEC CITY-4

Nom _______________ Classe _______________ Date _______________

Sports et passe-temps

DEUXIEME ETAPE Student Make-Up Assignments Checklist

Pupil's Edition, pp. 116–120

Study	Assignments
Study the expressions in the **Comment dit-on... ?** box on page 116: exchanging information. You should know how to find out a friend's interests and how to tell about yours.	☐ For additional practice, do Activities 4–5, p. 129 in the **Grammaire supplémentaire.**
Study the grammar presentation in the **Note de grammaire** box on page 116: the partitive in negation.	☐ Do Activity 14, p. 116 as a writing activity. Write a conversation between two friends talking about the sports and hobbies that they like. ☐ For additional practice, do Activity 4, p. 129 in the **Grammaire supplémentaire.** ☐ For additional practice, do Activity 10, p. 41 in the **Cahier d'activités.** ☐ For additional practice, do Activities 7–8, p. 28 in the **Travaux pratiques de grammaire.**
Study the grammar presentation in the **Grammaire** box on page 116: the verb **faire.**	☐ Do Activity 15, p. 116. ☐ Do Activity 16, p. 117 as a writing activity. ☐ For additional practice, do Activities 5–6, pp. 129–130 in the **Grammaire supplémentaire.** ☐ For additional practice, do Activity 11, p. 41 in the **Cahier d'activités.** ☐ For additional practice, do Activities 9–10, p. 29 in the **Travaux pratiques de grammaire.** ☐ For additional practice, do Activity 3, CD 1 in the **Interactive CD-ROM Tutor.**
Study the grammar presentation in the **Grammaire** box on page 117: the pronoun **on.**	☐ Do Activity 17, p. 117 as a writing activity. ☐ For additional practice, do Activity 7, p. 130 in the **Grammaire supplémentaire.** ☐ For additional practice, do Activity 9, p. 41 in the **Cahier d'activités.** ☐ For additional practice, do Activity 11, p. 30 in the **Travaux pratiques de grammaire.**

Study the **Vocabulaire** on page 118.	☐ Do Activity 18, p. 118 as a writing activity. ☐ Do Activity 19, p. 118. ☐ For additional practice, do Activity 12, p. 30 in the **Travaux pratiques de grammaire.**
Study the **Vocabulaire** on page 119.	☐ Do Activity 20, p. 119, as a writing activity. ☐ For additional practice, do Activity 17, p. 44 in the **Cahier d'activités.** ☐ For additional practice, do Activities 13–14, p. 31 in the **Travaux pratiques de grammaire.**
Study the **Vocabulaire** on page 120.	☐ Do Activity 23, p. 120 as a writing activity. ☐ Do Activity 25, p. 120. ☐ For additional practice, do Activities 12–14, p. 42 in the **Cahier d'activités.** ☐ For additional practice, do Activity 16, p. 32 in the **Travaux pratiques de grammaire.** ☐ For additional practice, do Activity 4, CD 1 in the **Interactive CD-ROM Tutor.**

DEUXIEME ETAPE Self-Test

Can you exchange information?	How would you tell someone about a few of your sports and hobbies, using the verbs **jouer** and **faire?** How would you find out if someone plays the games represented in the drawings in Activity 4 on the **Que sais-je?** page 134? How would you tell someone in French . . . 1. what you do in a certain season? 2. what you like to do in a certain month? 3. what you do in a certain weather? 4. what you like to do at a certain time of the day?

For an online self-test, go to go.hrw.com.

WA3 QUEBEC CITY-4

Nom_______________ Classe_______________ Date_______________

Sport et passe-temps

CHAPITRE 4

TROISIEME ETAPE Student Make-Up Assignments Checklist

Pupil's Edition, pp. 122–125

Study the expressions in the **Comment dit-on... ?** box on page 122: making, accepting, and turning down suggestions. You should know how to make, accept, and turn down a suggestion.	☐ Do Activity 27, p. 122 as a writing activity. Write a conversation in which you invite friends to do something with you. ☐ For additional practice, do Activity 19, p. 45 in the **Cahier d'activités.** ☐ For additional practice, do Activity 5, CD 1 in the **Interactive CD-ROM Tutor.**
Study the grammar presentation in the **Grammaire** box on page 122: adverbs of frequency.	☐ Do Activity 29, p. 123 as a writing activity. Write a short paragraph describing Pauline's calendar. ☐ Do Activity 30, p. 123 as a writing activity. Write conversation between two friends in which they talk about how often they practice their favorite pastimes. ☐ Do Activity 31, p. 124. ☐ Do Activity 32, p. 124 as a writing activity. ☐ Do Activity 33, p. 124. ☐ Do Activity 34, p. 125. ☐ Do Activity 35, p. 125. ☐ For additional practice, do Activities 9–10, p. 131 in the **Grammaire supplémentaire.** ☐ For additional practice, do Activities 20–22, pp. 45–46 in the **Cahier d'activités.** ☐ For additional practice, do Activities 18–20, p. 34 in the **Travaux pratiques de grammaire.** ☐ For additional practice, do Activity 6, CD 1 in the **Interactive CD-ROM Tutor.**

TROISIEME ETAPE Self-Test

Can you make, accept, and turn down suggestions?	How would you suggest that . . . 1. you and a friend go waterskiing? 2. you and your friends play baseball? If a friend asked you to go jogging, how would you accept the suggestion? How would you turn it down?

For an online self-test, go to **go.hrw.com**.

WA3 QUEBEC CITY-4

Nom _______________ Classe _______________ Date _______________

On va au café?

PREMIERE ETAPE Student Make-Up Assignments Checklist

Pupil's Edition, pp. 145–149

Study the expressions in the **Comment dit-on... ?** box on page 145: making suggestions; making excuses. You should know how to make suggestions and how to make excuses.	☐ Do Activity 7, p. 146 as a writing activity. ☐ Do Activity 8, p. 146. ☐ For additional practice, do Activities 7–8, pp. 51–52 in the **Cahier d'activités.**
Study the **Vocabulaire** on page 147.	☐ Do Activity 10, p. 148. ☐ Do Activity 11, p. 148. ☐ For additional practice, do Activity 3, p. 50 in the **Cahier d'activités.** ☐ For additional practice, do Activities 1–4, pp. 35–36 in the **Travaux pratiques de grammaire.** ☐ For additional practice, do Activities 1–2, CD 2 in the **Interactive CD-ROM Tutor.**
Study the expressions in the **Comment dit-on... ?** box on page 148: making a recommendation. You should know how to recommend something to eat or drink.	☐ For additional practice, do Activity 5, p. 36 in the **Travaux pratiques de grammaire.**
Study the grammar presentation in the **Grammaire** box on page 149: the verb **prendre.**	☐ Do Activity 12, p. 149. ☐ Do Activity 13, p. 149 as a writing activity. ☐ For additional practice, do Activities 1–2, p. 160 in the **Grammaire supplémentaire.** ☐ For additional practice, do Activity 5, p. 51 in the **Cahier d'activités.** ☐ For additional practice, do Activities 6–7, p. 37 in the **Travaux pratiques de grammaire.** ☐ For additional practice, do Activity 3, CD 2 in the **Interactive CD-ROM Tutor.**

PREMIERE ETAPE Self-Test

Can you make suggestions, excuses, and recommendations?	How would you suggest to a friend that you . . . 1. go to the café? 2. play tennis? How would you turn down a suggestion and make an excuse? How would you recommend to a friend something . . . 1. to eat? 2. to drink?

For an online self-test, go to **go.hrw.com**.

WA3 PARIS-5

CHAPITRE 5

Nom ______________________ Classe ______________ Date ______________

On va au café?

DEUXIEME ETAPE Student Make-Up Assignments Checklist

Pupil's Edition, pp. 151–153

Study the expressions in the **Comment dit-on... ?** box on page 151: getting someone's attention; ordering food and beverages. You should know how to get the server's attention, how to ask for what you want, how to order.	☐ Do Activity 15, p. 151 as a writing activity. ☐ Do Activity 16, p. 152 as a writing activity. Write a conversation. ☐ For additional practice, do Activities 10–12, p. 53 in the **Cahier d'activités.**
Study the grammar presentation in the **Grammaire** box on page 152: the imperative.	☐ Do Activity 17, p. 152 as a writing activity. ☐ Do Activity 18, p. 153 as a writing activity. Write a conversation. ☐ Do Activity 19, p. 153 as a writing activity. ☐ Do Activity 20, p. 153. ☐ For additional practice, do Activities 3–6, pp. 161–162 in the **Grammaire supplémentaire.** ☐ For additional practice, do Activities 13 and 15, p. 54 in the **Cahier d'activités.** ☐ For additional practice, do Activities 8–10, p. 38 in the **Travaux pratiques de grammaire.** ☐ For additional practice, do Activity 4, CD 2 in the **Interactive CD-ROM Tutor.**

DEUXIEME ETAPE Self-Test

Can you get someone's attention and order food and beverages?	In a café, how would you . . . 1. get the server's attention? 2. ask what kinds of sandwiches they serve? 3. ask what there is to drink? How would you say that you're . . . 1. hungry? 2. thirsty? How would you tell what people are having, using the verb **prendre?** Use the pronouns and the items in the drawings in Activity 7 in the **Que sais-je?** page 166.

For an online self-test, go to **go.hrw.com**.

WA3 PARIS-5

Nom________________ Classe____________ Date____________

On va au café?

TROISIEME ETAPE Student Make-Up Assignments Checklist

Pupil's Edition, pp. 154–157

Study the expressions in the **Comment dit-on... ?** box on page 154: inquiring about and expressing likes and dislikes. You should know how to ask if someone likes his/her food and say that you like or dislike your food.	☐ Do Activity 22, p. 154 as a writing activity. Write about how you like or dislike the items in the pictures. ☐ Do Activity 23, p. 155 as a writing activity. ☐ Do Activity 24, p. 155. ☐ For additional practice, do Activities 19–21, pp. 56–57 in the **Cahier d'activités.** ☐ For additional practice, do Activities 11–12, p. 39 in the **Travaux pratiques de grammaire.**
Study the expressions in the **Comment dit-on... ?** box on page 155: paying the check. You should know how to ask for the check or ask how much something is.	☐ Do Activity 26, p. 156 as a writing activity. ☐ Do Activity 27, p. 156. ☐ For additional practice, do Activity 7, p. 163 in the **Grammaire supplémentaire.** ☐ For additional practice, do Activities 23–24, pp. 57–58 in the **Cahier d'activités.** ☐ For additional practice, do Activities 5–6, CD 2 in the **Interactive CD-ROM Tutor.**

TROISIEME ETAPE Self-Test

Can you inquire about and express likes and dislikes?	How would you ask a friend if he or she likes a certain food? How would you tell someone what you think of the items represented in Activities 7 and 9 in the **Que sais-je?**, page 166?
Can you pay the check?	How would you ask how much each item in Activity 9 on the **Que sais-je?** page 166 costs? How would you ask for the check? How would you ask what the total is?

For an online self-test, go to **go.hrw.com**.

WA3 PARIS-5

Nom ______________________ Classe ______________ Date ______________

Amusons-nous!

PREMIERE ETAPE Student Make-Up Assignments Checklist

Pupil's Edition, pp. 173–177

Study the expressions in the **Comment dit-on... ?** box on page 173: making plans. You should know how to ask what a friend is planning to do and say what you are going to do.	☐ Do Part a. of Activity 8, p. 173 as a writing activity.
Study the grammar presentation in the **Note de grammaire** box on page 173: one-time activities versus regularly scheduled ones.	☐ For additional practice, do Activities 1–2, p. 190 in the **Grammaire supplémentaire.** ☐ For additional practice, do Activities 3–4, p. 42 in the **Travaux pratiques de grammaire.**
Study the **Vocabulaire** on page 173.	☐ For additional practice, do Activities 1–2, p. 41 in the **Travaux pratiques de grammaire.**
Study the grammar presentation in the **Grammaire** box on page 174: the verb **aller.**	☐ Do Activity 10, p. 174 as a writing activity. ☐ Do Activity 11, p. 175. ☐ For additional practice, do Activities 3–4, p. 191 in the **Grammaire supplémentaire.** ☐ For additional practice, do Activity 7, p. 63 in the **Cahier d'activités.** ☐ For additional practice, do Activities 5–6, p. 43 in the **Travaux pratiques de grammaire.** ☐ For additional practice, do Activity 1, CD 2 in the **Interactive CD-ROM Tutor.**

Nom ____________________ Classe ____________ Date ____________

Study the **Vocabulaire** on page 176.	☐ Do Activity 13, p. 176 as a writing activity. ☐ For additional practice, do Activities 6 and 8, pp. 63–64 in the **Cahier d'activités.** ☐ For additional practice, do Activities 7–9, pp. 44–45 in the **Travaux pratiques de grammaire.** ☐ For additional practice, do Activities 2–3, CD 2 in the **Interactive CD-ROM Tutor.**
Study the grammar presentation in the **Grammaire** box on page 177: contractions with **à.**	☐ Do Activity 14, p. 177. ☐ Do Activity 15, p. 177 as a writing activity. Write a conversation. ☐ Do Activity 16, p. 177. ☐ For additional practice, do Activities 5–6, pp. 191–192 in the **Grammaire supplémentaire**. ☐ For additional practice, do Activities 10–11, p. 45 in the **Travaux pratiques de grammaire.**

PREMIERE ETAPE Self-Test

Can you make plans?	How would you say that the people in the drawings in Activity 1 on the **Que sais-je?** page 196 are going to these places? How would you tell what you're planning to do this weekend?

For an online self-test, go to go.hrw.com.

WA3 PARIS-6

CHAPITRE 6

Nom_______________ Classe___________ Date___________

Amusons-nous!

DEUXIEME ETAPE Student Make-Up Assignments Checklist

Pupil's Edition, pp. 179–181

Study the expressions in the **Comment dit-on... ?** box on page 179: extending and responding to invitations. You should know how to extend, accept, and refuse an invitation.	☐ Do Activity 18, p. 180 as a writing activity. ☐ Do Activity 19, p. 180 as a writing activity. Write a conversation using the clues in the activity. ☐ For additional practice, do Activities 11–14, pp. 65–66 in the **Cahier d'activités.** ☐ For additional practice, do Activity 4, CD 2 in the **Interactive CD-ROM Tutor.**
Study the grammar presentation in the **Grammaire** box on page 180: the verb **vouloir.**	☐ Do Activity 20, p. 181 as a writing activity. ☐ Do Activity 21, p. 181 as a writing activity. Write a conversation using the clues from the activity. ☐ Do Activity 22, p. 181 as a writing activity. Write a conversation using the clues from the activity. ☐ Do Activity 23, p. 181 as a writing activity. Write a conversation using the clues from the activity. ☐ For additional practice, do Activities 7–8, p. 192 in the **Grammaire supplémentaire.** ☐ For additional practice, do Activities 15–16, pp. 66–67 in the **Cahier d'activités.** ☐ For additional practice, do Activities 12–13, p. 46 in the **Travaux pratiques de grammaire.** ☐ For additional practice, do Activity 5, CD 2 in the **Interactive CD-ROM Tutor.**

Nom ______________________ Classe ______________ Date ______________

DEUXIEME ETAPE Self-Test

Can you extend and respond to invitations?	How would you invite a friend to . . . 1. go window shopping? 2. go for a walk? 3. go see a basketball game? 4. go to the café? How would you accept the following invitations? How would you refuse them? 1. Je voudrais aller faire du ski. Tu viens? 2. Allons à la Maison des jeunes! 3. On va au restaurant. Tu viens? 4. Tu veux aller au cinéma? How would you say that the following people want to go to the places in the drawings in Activity 5 on the **Que sais-je?** page 196?

For an online self-test, go to **go.hrw.com**.

WA3 PARIS-6

CHAPITRE 6

Nom ________________ Classe ____________ Date ____________

Amusons-nous!

TROISIEME ETAPE Student Make-Up Assignments Checklist

Pupil's Edition, pp. 183–187

Study the expressions in the **Comment dit-on... ?** box on page 183: arranging to meet someone. You should know how to arrange to meet someone.	☐ Do Activity 25, p. 184 as a writing activity. ☐ Do Part a. of Activity 27, p. 185 ☐ For additional practice, do Activities 19–20, pp. 68–69 in the **Cahier d'activités.** ☐ For additional practice, do Activities 14–17, pp. 47–48 in the **Travaux pratiques de grammaire.** ☐ For additional practice, do Activity 6, CD 2 in the **Interactive CD-ROM Tutor.**
Study the grammar presentation in the **Grammaire** box on page 185: information questions.	☐ Do Activity 28, p. 185 as a writing activity. Use the clues from the activity. ☐ Do Activity 29, p. 186. ☐ Do Activity 30, p. 186 as a writing activity. Use the clues from the activity. ☐ Do Activity 31, p. 186. ☐ For additional practice, do Activities 9–10, p. 193 in the **Grammaire supplémentaire.** ☐ For additional practice, do Activities 21–22, p. 69 in the **Cahier d'activités.** ☐ For additional practice, do Activities 18–21, pp. 49–50 in the **Travaux pratiques de grammaire.**

TROISIEME ETAPE Self-Test

Can you arrange to meet someone?	If someone invited you to go to the movies, what are three questions you might ask to find out more information?
	What are some possible answers to the following questions? 1. Où ça? 2. Avec qui? 3. A quelle heure? 4. Quand ça?

For an online self-test, go to go.hrw.com.

WA3 PARIS-6

CHAPITRE 6

Nom _______________ Classe _______________ Date _______________

La famille

PREMIERE ETAPE Student Make-Up Assignments Checklist

Pupil's Edition, pp. 203–207

Study the expressions in the **Comment dit-on... ?** box on page 203: identifying people. You should know how to identify people.	☐ Do Activity 6, p. 203 as a writing activity.
Study the **Vocabulaire** on page 204.	☐ For additional practice, do Activities 2a, 4, pp. 74–75 in the **Cahier d'activités.** ☐ For additional practice, do Activities 1–2, p. 51 in the **Travaux pratiques de grammaire.** ☐ For additional practice, do Activity 1, CD 2 in the **Interactive CD-ROM Tutor.**
Study the grammar presentation in the **Note de grammaire** box on page 204: the preposition **de** to indicate relationship or ownership.	☐ Do Activity 7, p. 204 as a writing activity. ☐ For additional practice, do Activities 2b, 7b, pp. 74, 76 in the **Cahier d'activités.** ☐ For additional practice, do Activities 3–4, p. 52 in the **Travaux pratiques de grammaire.**
Study the grammar presentation in the **Grammaire** box on page 205: possessive adjectives.	☐ Do Activity 10, p. 206 as a writing activity. ☐ Do Activity 11, p. 206 as a writing activity. ☐ For additional practice, do Activities 2–4, pp. 218–219 in the **Grammaire supplémentaire.** ☐ For additional practice, do Activities 6–7a, pp. 75–76 in the **Cahier d'activités.** ☐ For additional practice, do Activities 5–7, p. 53 in the **Travaux pratiques de grammaire.**
Study the expressions in the **Comment dit-on... ?** box on page 207: introducing people. You should know how to introduce someone to a friend and to an adult and how to respond to an introduction.	☐ Do Activity 13, p. 207 as a writing activity. ☐ Do Activity 14, p. 207. ☐ For additional practice, do Activity 8, p. 76 in the **Cahier d'activités.**

PREMIERE ETAPE Self-Test

Can you identify people?	How would you point out and identify Isabelle's relatives? How would you give their names and approximate ages? See page 204. 1. her grandparents 2. her uncle 3. her cousin Loïc 4. her brother
Can you introduce people?	How would you introduce your friend to . . . 1. an adult relative? 2. a classmate?

For an online self-test, go to **go.hrw.com**.

WA3 PARIS-7

Nom ____________________ Classe ____________ Date ____________

La famille

DEUXIEME ETAPE Student Make-Up Assignments Checklist

Pupil's Edition, pp. 208–211

Study the **Vocabulaire** on page 208.	☐ For additional practice, do Activities 9–10, p. 77 in the **Cahier d'activités.** ☐ For additional practice, do Activities 8–9, p. 54 in the **Travaux pratiques de grammaire.**
Study the expressions in the **Comment dit-on... ?** box on page 209: describing and characterizing people. You should know how to ask what someone is like, describe, and characterize someone.	☐ Do Activity 17, p. 209 as a writing activity. ☐ For additional practice, do Activity 13, p. 78 in the **Cahier d'activités.**
Study the grammar presentation in the **Grammaire** box on page 210: adjective agreement.	☐ Do Activity 18, p. 210 as a writing activity. ☐ Do Activity 19, p. 210 as a writing activity. ☐ For additional practice, do Activities 5–8, pp. 219–220 in the **Grammaire supplémentaire.** ☐ For additional practice, do Activities 11–12, pp. 77–78 in the **Cahier d'activités.** ☐ For additional practice, do Activities 10–14, pp. 55–57 in the **Travaux pratiques de grammaire.** ☐ For additional practice, do Activity 2, CD 2 in the **Interactive CD-ROM Tutor.**

Study the grammar presentation in the **Grammaire** box on page 211: the verb **être**.

- ☐ Do Activity 20, p. 211.
- ☐ Do the first part of Activity 21, p. 211 as a writing activity. Write a description of a member of the Louvain family.
- ☐ Do Activity 22, p. 211.
- ☐ For additional practice, do Activities 14–15, pp. 78–79 in the **Cahier d'activités.**
- ☐ For additional practice, do Activities 15–17, pp. 57–58 in the **Travaux pratiques de grammaire.**
- ☐ For additional practice, do Activity 4, CD 2 in the **Interactive CD-ROM Tutor.**

DEUXIEME ETAPE Self-Test

Can you describe and characterize people?

How would you describe the people in the drawings on the **Que sais-je?** page 224?

How would you . . .

1. tell a friend that he or she is nice?
2. tell several friends that they're annoying?
3. say that you and your friend are intelligent?

For an online self-test, go to go.hrw.com.

WA3 PARIS-7

Nom ______________________ Classe ______________ Date ______________

La famille

TROISIEME ETAPE Student Make-Up Assignments Checklist

Pupil's Edition, pp. 213–215

Study the expressions in the **Comment dit-on... ?** box on page 213: asking for, giving, and refusing permission. You should know how to ask for, give, and refuse permission.

- ☐ Do Activity 25, p. 214 as a writing activity. Write about the chores at your home.
- ☐ Do Activity 26, p. 214.
- ☐ Do Activity 27, p. 215 as a writing activity.
- ☐ For additional practice, do Activity 10, p. 221 in the **Grammaire supplémentaire.**
- ☐ For additional practice, do Activity 21, p. 81 in the **Cahier d'activités.**
- ☐ For additional practice, do Activity 5, CD 2 in the **Interactive CD-ROM Tutor.**

Study the **Vocabulaire** on page 213.

- ☐ For additional practice, do Activity 11, p. 221 in the **Grammaire supplémentaire.**
- ☐ For additional practice, do Activities 17–18, 20, 22–23, pp. 80–82 in the **Cahier d'activités.**
- ☐ For additional practice, do Activities 18–21, pp. 59–60 in the **Travaux pratiques de grammaire.**
- ☐ For additional practice, do Activity 6, CD 2 in the **Interactive CD-ROM Tutor.**

TROISIEME ETAPE Self-Test

Can you ask for, give, and refuse permission?	How would you ask permission to . . . 1. go to the movies? 2. go out with your friends? 3. go shopping? 4. go ice-skating? How would you give someone permission to do something? How would you refuse? What are three things your parents might ask you to do before allowing you to go out with your friends?

For an online self-test, go to **go.hrw.com**.

WA3 PARIS-7

CHAPITRE 8

Nom ______ Classe ______ Date ______

Au marché

PREMIERE ETAPE Student Make-Up Assignments Checklist

Pupil's Edition, pp. 235–238

Study the **Vocabulaire** on page 235.	☐ For additional practice, do Activities 3–5, pp. 86–87 in the **Cahier d'activités.** ☐ For additional practice, do Activities 1–4, pp. 61–62 in the **Travaux pratiques de grammaire.** ☐ For additional practice, do Activities 1–2, CD 2 in the **Interactive CD-ROM Tutor.**
Study the grammar presentation in the **Grammaire** box on page 236: the partitive and indefinite articles.	☐ Do Activity 8, p. 236. ☐ Do Activity 9, p. 237 as a writing activity. ☐ For additional practice, do Activities 1–3, p. 252 in the **Grammaire supplémentaire.** ☐ For additional practice, do Activity 6, p. 87 in the **Cahier d'activités.** ☐ For additional practice, do Activities 5–9, pp. 63–65 in the **Travaux pratiques de grammaire.** ☐ For additional practice, do Activity 3, CD 2 in the **Interactive CD-ROM Tutor.**
Study the expressions in the **Comment dit-on... ?** box on page 238: expressing need. You should know how to ask your friend what he or she needs and say what you need.	☐ For additional practice, do Activity 8, p. 88 in the **Cahier d'activités.**
Study the grammar presentation in the **Note de grammaire** box on page 238: the expression **avoir besoin de.**	☐ Do Activity 11, p. 238 as a writing activity. ☐ Do Activity 12, p. 238. ☐ Do Activity 13, p. 238 as a writing activity. Write a conversation based on the clues from the activity. ☐ For additional practice, do Activity 4, p. 253 in the **Grammaire supplémentaire.** ☐ For additional practice, do Activity 9, p. 88 in the **Cahier d'activités.** ☐ For additional practice, do Activity 10, p. 65 in the **Travaux pratiques de grammaire.**

Nom ______________________ Classe ______________ Date ______________

PREMIERE ETAPE Self-Test

Can you express need?	How would you tell someone that you need the items in the drawings in Activity 1 on the **Que sais-je?** page 258?

For an online self-test, go to **go.hrw.com**.

WA3 ABIDJAN-8

CHAPITRE 8

Nom______________________ Classe______________ Date______________

Au marché

DEUXIEME ETAPE Student Make-Up Assignments Checklist

Pupil's Edition, pp. 240–243

Study the expressions in the **Comment dit-on... ?** box on page 240: making, accepting, and declining requests; telling someone what to do. You should know how to make, accept, and decline requests and how to tell someone what to do.	☐ For additional practice, do Activities 10–12, p. 89 in the **Cahier d'activités.**
Study the grammar presentation in the **Grammaire** box on page 241: the verb **pouvoir.**	☐ Do Activity 15, p. 241. ☐ Do Activity 16, p. 241 as a writing activity. Write a conversation using the clues in the activity. ☐ For additional practice, do Activities 5–6, p. 253 in the **Grammaire supplémentaire.** ☐ For additional practice, do Activities 13–14, p. 90 in the **Cahier d'activités.** ☐ For additional practice, do Activities 11–12, p. 66 in the **Travaux pratiques de grammaire.** ☐ For additional practice, do Activity 4, CD 2 in the **Interactive CD-ROM Tutor.**
Study the **Vocabulaire** on page 242.	☐ Do Activity 18, p. 243. ☐ For additional practice, do Activities 15–17, pp. 90–91 in the **Cahier d'activités.** ☐ For additional practice, do Activity 13, p. 67 in the **Travaux pratiques de grammaire.** ☐ For additional practice, do Activity 5, CD 2 in the **Interactive CD-ROM Tutor.**

Study the grammar presentation in the **Note de grammaire** box on page 242: **de** in expressions of quantity.

- ☐ Do Activity 19, p. 243 as a writing activity. Write a conversation based on the clues in the activity.
- ☐ Do Activity 20, p. 243 as a writing activity. Write a conversation based on the clues in the activity.
- ☐ For additional practice, do Activity 8, p. 254 in the **Grammaire supplémentaire.**
- ☐ For additional practice, do Activities 14–16, pp. 67–68 in the **Travaux pratiques de grammaire.**

DEUXIEME ETAPE Self-Test

Can you make, accept, and decline requests or tell someone what to do?

How would you . . .

1. ask someone to go grocery shopping for you?
2. tell someone to bring back some groceries for you?

How would you accept the requests in the previous activity? How would you refuse?

How would you ask for a specific quantity of these foods?

1. œufs
2. lait
3. oranges
4. beurre
5. jambon
6. eau minérale

For an online self-test, go to go.hrw.com.

WA3 ABIDJAN-8

Nom ______________________ Classe ______________ Date ______________

CHAPITRE 8

Au marché

TROISIEME ETAPE Student Make-Up Assignments Checklist

Pupil's Edition, pp. 245–249

Study the **Vocabulaire** on page 245.	☐ Do Activity 22, p. 246 as a writing activity. ☐ Do Activity 23, p. 247 as a writing activity. ☐ Do Activity 24, p. 247. Do the first part only. ☐ For additional practice, do Activities 19–20, p. 92 in the **Cahier d'activités.** ☐ For additional practice, do Activities 17–18, p. 69 in the **Travaux pratiques de grammaire.**
Study the expressions in the **Comment dit-on... ?** box on page 247: offering, accepting, or refusing food. You should know how to offer, accept, or refuse food.	☐ Do Activity 26, p. 248 as a writing activity. Write a conversation based on the clues in the activity. ☐ For additional practice, do Activities 21–22, pp. 92–93 in the **Cahier d'activités.** ☐ For additional practice, do Activity 6, CD 2 in the **Interactive CD-ROM Tutor.**
Study the grammar presentation in the **Grammaire** box on page 248: the pronoun **en.**	☐ Do Activity 27, p. 248. ☐ Do Activity 28, p. 249 as a writing activity. Write a conversatin based on the clues in the activity. ☐ Do Activity 29, p. 249. ☐ For additional practice, do Activities 9–11, pp. 254–255 in the **Grammaire supplémentaire.** ☐ For additional practice, do Activity 23, p. 93 in the **Cahier d'activités.** ☐ For additional practice, do Activities 19–20, p. 70 in the **Travaux pratiques de grammaire.**

Nom ______________________ Classe ______________ Date ______________

TROISIEME ETAPE Self-Test

Can you offer, accept, or refuse food?	How would you offer someone these foods? 1. some rice 2. some oranges 3. some milk How would you accept the food listed in the previous activity if they were offered? How would you refuse them? How would you tell someone what you have for . . . 1. breakfast? 2. lunch? 3. an afternoon snack? 4. dinner?

CHAPITRE 8

For an online self-test, go to **go.hrw.com**.

WA3 ABIDJAN-8

CHAPITRE 9

Nom_______________ Classe_______________ Date_______________

Au téléphone

PREMIERE ETAPE Student Make-Up Assignments Checklist

Pupil's Edition, pp. 269–274

Study the expressions in the **Comment dit-on... ?** box on page 269: asking for and expressing opinions. You should know how to ask for someone's opinion, express indifference, express satisfaction and dissatisfaction.	☐ Do Activity 8, p. 269 as a writing activity. Write about your weekend. ☐ For additional practice, do Activity 2, p. 98 in the **Cahier d'activités.**
Study the expressions in the **Comment dit-on... ?** box on page 270: inquiring about and relating past events. You should know how to inquire about and relate past events.	☐ Do Activity 9, p. 270 as a writing activity. ☐ For additional practice, do Activity 3, p. 98 in the **Cahier d'activités.**
Study the grammar presentation in the **Grammaire** box on page 271: the **passé composé** with **avoir.**	☐ Do Activity 11, p. 271 as a writing activity. ☐ Do Activity 12, p. 272 as a writing activity. Write about what you did and did not do this weekend. ☐ For additional practice, do Activities 1–3, pp. 284–285 in the **Grammaire supplémentaire.** ☐ For additional practice, do Activities 4, 6–7, pp. 98–99 in the **Cahier d'activités.** ☐ For additional practice, do Activities 1–7, pp. 71–74 in the **Travaux pratiques de grammaire.** ☐ For additional practice, do Activity 1, CD 3 in the **Interactive CD-ROM Tutor.**
Study the grammar presentation in the **Note de grammaire** box on page 272: the **passé composé** and adverb placement.	☐ Do Activity 13, p. 272 as a writing activity. ☐ For additional practice, do Activities 4–5, p. 285 in the **Grammaire supplémentaire.** ☐ For additional practice, do Activity 8, p. 74 in the **Travaux pratiques de grammaire.**

Nom ______________________ Classe ______________ Date ______________

Study the **Vocabulaire** on page 273.	☐ Do Activity 14, p. 274 as a writing activity. ☐ Do Activity 15, p. 274 as a writing activity. ☐ Do Activity 16, p. 274. Do the first part only. ☐ Do Activity 17, p. 274. ☐ For additional practice, do Activities 9–10, p. 75 in the **Travaux pratiques de grammaire.** ☐ For additional practice, do Activities 2–3, CD 3 in the **Interactive CD-ROM Tutor.**

PREMIERE ETAPE Self-Test

Can you ask for and express opinions?	How would you ask a friend how his or her weekend went? How would you tell someone that your weekend was . . . 1. great? 2. OK? 3. horrible?
Can you inquire about and relate past events?	If you were inquiring about your friend's weekend, how would you ask . . . 1. what your friend did? 2. where your friend went? 3. what happened? How would you tell someone that you did the things in the drawings in Activity 4 on the **Que sais-je?** page 290?

CHAPITRE 9

For an online self-test, go to go.hrw.com.

WA3 ARLES-9

Nom_______________ Classe_______________ Date_______________

Au téléphone

DEUXIEME ETAPE Student Make-Up Assignments Checklist

Pupil's Edition, pp. 275–277

Study the expressions in the **Comment dit-on... ?** box on page 276: making and answering a telephone call. You should know how to make and answer a phone call.	☐ Do Activity 20, p. 277 as a writing activity. ☐ Do Activity 22, p. 277 as a writing activity. Write the conversation between you and your friend's parent. ☐ For additional practice, do Activities 13–14, p. 102 in the **Cahier d'activités.** ☐ For additional practice, do Activities 11–12, p. 76 in the **Travaux pratiques de grammaire.** ☐ For additional practice, do Activities 4–5, CD 3 in the **Interactive CD-ROM Tutor.**
Study the grammar presentation in the **Grammaire** box on page 277: **-re** verbs.	☐ Do Activity 23, p. 277. ☐ For additional practice, do Activities 6–8, p. 286 in the **Grammaire supplémentaire.** ☐ For additional practice, do Activities 15–16, p. 103 in the **Cahier d'activités.** ☐ For additional practice, do Activities 13–14, p. 77 in the **Travaux pratiques de grammaire.**

DEUXIEME ETAPE Self-Test

Can you make and answer a telephone call?	If you were answering a telephone call, how would you . . . 1. tell who you are? 2. ask if it's the right house? 3. ask to speak to someone? 4. ask to leave a message? 5. ask someone to say you called? 6. tell someone the line's busy? If you were answering a telephone call, how would you . . . 1. ask who's calling? 2. ask someone to hold? 3. ask someone to call back later?

For an online self-test, go to **go.hrw.com**.

WA3 ARLES-9

Nom______________________ Classe______________ Date______________

Au téléphone

TROISIEME ETAPE Student Make-Up Assignments Checklist

Pupil's Edition, pp. 279–281

Study the expressions in the **Comment dit-on... ?** box on page 279: sharing confidences and consoling others; asking for and giving advice. You should know how to share a confidence, console someone, ask for and give advice.	☐ For additional practice, do Activities 18–22, pp. 104–105 in the **Cahier d'activités.** ☐ For additional practice, do Activity 6, CD 3 in the **Interactive CD-ROM Tutor.**
Study the grammar presentation in the **Note de grammaire** box on page 279: pronouns.	☐ Do Activity 26, p. 280 as a writing activity. ☐ Do Activity 27, p. 280. ☐ Do Activity 28, p. 280 as a writing activity. Write the conversation based on the clues in the activity. ☐ Do Activity 29, p. 280 as a writing activity. Write the conversation based on the clues in the activity. ☐ For additional practice, do Activities 9–10, p. 287 in the **Grammaire supplémentaire.** ☐ For additional practice, do Activities 15–16, p. 78 in the **Travaux pratiques de grammaire.**

TROISIEME ETAPE Self-Test

Can you share confidences, console others, and ask for and give advice?	How would you approach a friend about a problem you have?
	What would you say to console a friend?
	How would you ask a friend for advice?
	How would you tell a friend what you think he or she should do?

For an online self-test, go to **go.hrw.com**.

WA3 ARLES-9

Nom ______________________ Classe ______________ Date ______________

CHAPITRE 10

Dans un magasin de vêtements

PREMIERE ETAPE Student Make-Up Assignments Checklist

Pupil's Edition, pp. 297–300

Study the **Vocabulaire** on page 297.	☐ Do Activity 8, p. 298 as a writing activity. ☐ Do Activity 9, p. 298. ☐ Do Activity 10, p. 298 as a writing activity. ☐ For additional practice, do Activities 2–4, p. 110 in the **Cahier d'activités.** ☐ For additional practice, do Activities 1–3, pp. 79–80 in the **Travaux pratiques de grammaire.** ☐ For additional practice, do Activities 1–2, CD 3 in the **Interactive CD-ROM Tutor.**
Study the grammar presentation in the **Grammaire** box on page 299: the verbs **mettre** and **porter.**	☐ Do Activity 11, p. 299 as a writing activity. ☐ Do Activity 12, p. 299 as a writing activity. Write about yourself. ☐ For additional practice, do Activities 1–3, p. 314 in the **Grammaire supplémentaire.** ☐ For additional practice, do Activities 6–7, p. 111 in the **Cahier d'activités.** ☐ For additional practice, do Activities 4–6, pp. 80–81 in the **Travaux pratiques de grammaire.**
Study the expressions in the **Comment dit-on... ?** box on page 300: asking for and giving advice. You should know how to ask for and give advice.	☐ Do Activity14, p. 300 as a writing activity. ☐ Do Activity 15, p. 300 as a writing activity. ☐ Do Activity 16, p. 300. ☐ For additional practice, do Activities 8–9, p. 112 in the **Cahier d'activités.**

Nom ______________________ Classe ______________ Date ______________

CHAPITRE 10

PREMIERE ETAPE Self-Test

Can you ask for and give advice?	How would you ask a friend what you should wear to a party?
	How would you advise a friend to wear the clothes in the pictures in Activity 2 on the **Que sais-je?** page 320 using the verb **mettre?**

For an online self-test, go to go.hrw.com.

WA3 ARLES-10

CHAPITRE 10

Nom ______________ Classe ______________ Date ______________

Dans un magasin de vêtements

CHAPITRE 10

DEUXIEME ETAPE Student Make-Up Assignments Checklist

Pupil's Edition, pp. 301–304

Study the expressions in the **Comment dit-on... ?** box on page 301: expressing need; inquiring. You should know how to express what you need and inquire about prices, sizes, colors, and fabrics.	☐ For additional practice, do Activities 10–11, p. 113 in the **Cahier d'activités.** ☐ For additional practice, do Activity 7, p. 82 in the **Travaux pratiques de grammaire.**
Study the grammar presentation in the **Note de grammaire** box on page 301: adjectives used as nouns.	☐ Do Activity 19, p. 302 as a writing activity. Rewrite the sentences in the right order. ☐ Do Activity 20, p. 302. ☐ Do Activity 21, p. 302 as a writing activity. Write a conversation based on the clues from the activity. ☐ Do Activity 22, p. 303 as a writing activity. Write a conversation based on the clues from the activity. ☐ For additional practice, do Activity 4, p. 315 in the **Grammaire supplémentaire.** ☐ For additional practice, do Activity 12, p. 114 in the **Cahier d'activités.** ☐ For additional practice, do Activity 8, p. 82 in the **Travaux pratiques de grammaire.**
Study the grammar presentation in the **Grammaire** box on page 303: the **-ir** verbs.	☐ Do Activity 23, p. 304 as a writing activity. ☐ Do Activity 24, p. 304 as a writing activity. ☐ Do Activity 25, p. 304 as a writing activity. Write a conversation based on the clues from the activity. ☐ For additional practice, do Activities 5–7, pp. 315–316 in the **Grammaire supplémentaire.** ☐ For additional practice, do Activities 14–16, p. 115 in the **Cahier d'activités.** ☐ For additional practice, do Activities 9–12, pp. 83– 84 in the **Travaux pratiques de grammaire.** ☐ For additional practice, do Activity 3, CD 3 in the **Interactive CD-ROM Tutor.**

DEUXIEME ETAPE Self-Test

Can you express need and inquire?	How would you tell a salesperson . . . 1. that you're just looking? 2. what you would like? How would you ask a salesperson . . . 1. if you can try something on? 2. if they have what you want in a different size? 3. if they have what you want in a particular color? 4. how much something costs? How would you tell what the people are choosing based on the drawings in Activity 5 on the **Que sais-je?** page 320?

For an online self-test, go to **go.hrw.com**.

WA3 ARLES-10

Nom ______________ Classe ______________ Date ______________

Dans un magasin de vêtements

TROISIEME ETAPE Student Make-Up Assignments Checklist

Pupil's Edition, pp. 306–311

Study the expressions in the **Comment dit-on... ?** box on page 306: asking for an opinion, paying a compliment, and criticizing. You should know how to ask for an opinion, pay a compliment, or criticize.	☐ Do Activity 27, p. 306 as a writing activity. ☐ Do Activity 29, p. 309 as a writing activity. Write a conversation between two friends that are complimenting each other. ☐ For additional practice, do Activities 17–19, pp. 116–117 in the **Cahier d'activités.** ☐ For additional practice, do Activities 13–15, pp. 85–86 in the **Travaux pratiques de grammaire.** ☐ For additional practice, do Activity 5, CD 3 in the **Interactive CD-ROM Tutor.**
Study the grammar presentation in the **Grammaire** box on page 309: the direct object pronouns **le, la,** and **les.**	☐ Do Activity 30, p. 309. ☐ For additional practice, do Activities 8–9, pp. 316–317 in the **Grammaire supplémentaire.** ☐ For additional practice, do Activity 21, p. 117 in the **Cahier d'activités.** ☐ For additional practice, do Activities 16–17, pp. 86–87 in the **Travaux pratiques de grammaire.** ☐ For additional practice, do Activity 4, CD 3 in the **Interactive CD-ROM Tutor.**
Study the expressions in the **Comment dit-on... ?** box on page 310: hesitating; making a decision. You should know how to express hesitation and how to talk about making a decision.	☐ For additional practice, do Activity 22, p. 118 in the **Cahier d'activités.**

Study the grammar presentation in the **Note de grammaire** box on page 310: **il/elle est...** versus **c'est...**

- ☐ Do the first part of Activity 32, p. 310.
- ☐ Do Activity 33, p. 311 as a writing activity. Write a conversation using the clues on the activity.
- ☐ For additional practice, do Activity 10, p. 317 in the **Grammaire supplémentaire.**
- ☐ For additional practice, do Activity 23, p. 118 in the **Cahier d'activités.**
- ☐ For additional practice, do Activity 18, p. 87 in the **Travaux pratiques de grammaire.**
- ☐ For additional practice, do Activity 6, CD 3 in the **Interactive CD-ROM Tutor.**

TROISIEME ETAPE Self-Test

Can you ask for an opinion, pay a compliment, and criticize?

If you were shopping with a friend, how would you ask . . .

1. if your friend likes what you have on?
2. if something fits?
3. if it's too short?

How would you compliment a friend's clothing? How would you criticize it?

Can you hesitate and make a decision?

How can you express your hesitation?

How would you tell a salesperson what you've decided to do?

For an online self-test, go to go.hrw.com.

WA3 ARLES-10

CHAPITRE 11

Nom _______________ Classe _______________ Date _______________

Vive les vacances!

PREMIERE ETAPE Student Make-Up Assignments Checklist

Pupil's Edition, pp. 327–331

Study the **Vocabulaire** on page 327.	☐ Do Activity 7, p. 328 as a writing activity. ☐ For additional practice, do Activity 2, p. 122 in the **Cahier d'activités.** ☐ For additional practice, do Activities 1–4, pp. 88–89 in the **Travaux pratiques de grammaire.** ☐ For additional practice, do Activity 1, CD 3 in the **Interactive CD-ROM Tutor.**
Study the expressions in the **Comment dit-on... ?** box on page 329: inquiring about and sharing future plans; expressing indecision; expressing wishes. You should know how to inquire about someone's plans and share yours, and how to express indecision and wishes.	☐ Do Activity 9, p. 329 as a writing activity. Write a conversation based on the clues from the activity. ☐ For additional practice, do Activity 6, p. 123 in the **Cahier d'activités.**
Study the grammar presentation in the **Note de grammaire** box on page 330: the preposition **à.**	☐ Do Activity 10, p. 330 as a writing activity. Write complete sentences. ☐ Do Activity 11, p. 330 as a writing activity. ☐ Do Activity 12, p. 330 as a writing activity. ☐ Do Activity 14, p. 331 as a writing activity. ☐ Do Activity 15, p. 331 as a writing activity. Write a conversation based on the clues from the activity. ☐ Do Activity 16, p. 331. ☐ For additional practice, do Activity 3, p. 342 in the **Grammaire supplémentaire.** ☐ For additional practice, do Activity 7, p. 91 in the **Travaux pratiques de grammaire.**

CHAPITRE 11

Nom ______________________ Classe ______________ Date ______________

PREMIERE ETAPE Self-Test

Can you inquire about and share future plans?	How would you ask where a friend is going on vacation and what he or she is going to do? How would you answer these questions? 1. Où est-ce que tu vas aller pendant les vacances? 2. Qu'est-ce que tu vas faire?
Express indecision and wishes?	How would you tell someone . . . 1. you're not sure what to do? 2. where you'd really like to go?
Can you ask for advice? Make, accept, and refuse suggestions?	How would you ask a friend for advice about your vacation? How would you suggest to a friend that he or she . . . 1. go to the country? 2. go camping? 3. work? 4. go to Canada? How would you accept or refuse the suggestions in the previous activity?

CHAPITRE 11

For an online self-test, go to go.hrw.com.

WA3 ARLES-11

CHAPITRE 11

Nom _______________ Classe _______________ Date _______________

Vive les vacances!

DEUXIEME ETAPE Student Make-Up Assignments Checklist

Pupil's Edition, pp. 333–336

Study the **Vocabulaire** on page 333.	☐ Do Activity 17, p. 333 as a writing activity. ☐ For additional practice, do Activities 10–11, p. 125 in the **Cahier d'activités.** ☐ For additional practice, do Activities 8–9, p. 92 in the **Travaux pratiques de grammaire.** ☐ For additional practice, do Activity 2, CD 3 in the **Interactive CD-ROM Tutor.**
Study the expressions in the **Comment dit-on... ?** box on page 333: reminding; reassuring. You should know how to remind someone of something and reassure someone.	☐ Do Activity 19, p. 334 as a writing activity. Write the conversation between Jean-Paul and his parent. ☐ Do Activity 20, p. 334 as a writing activity. Write a conversation based on the clues from the activity. ☐ For additional practice, do Activity 13, p. 126 in the **Cahier d'activités.**
Study the grammar presentation in the **Grammaire** box on page 334: the verb **partir.**	☐ Do Activity 21, p. 335. ☐ Do Activity 22, p. 335 as a writing activity. ☐ Do Activity 23, p. 335 as a writing activity. Write a conversation based on the clues from the activity. ☐ Do Activity 24, p. 335. ☐ For additional practice, do Activities 6–8, p. 344 in the **Grammaire supplémentaire.** ☐ For additional practice, do Activity 12, p. 125 in the **Cahier d'activités.** ☐ For additional practice, do Activities 11–12, pp. 93–94 in the **Travaux pratiques de grammaire.** ☐ For additional practice, do Activity 3, CD 3 in the **Interactive CD-ROM Tutor.**

Nom ______________________ Classe ______________ Date ______________

Study the expressions in the **Comment dit-on... ?** box on page 336: seeing someone off. You should know how to wish someone a good trip.	☐ Do Activity 26, p. 336 as a writing activity. Write a conversation based on the clues from the activity. ☐ Do Activity 27, p. 336 as a writing activity. Write a conversation based on the clues from the activity. ☐ Do Activity 28, p. 336. ☐ For additional practice, do Activities 14–16, p. 127 in the **Cahier d'activités.**

DEUXIEME ETAPE Self-Test

Can you remind and reassure someone?	How would you remind a friend to take the items in the drawings in Activity 6 on the **Que sais-je?** page 348 on a trip? How would you reassure someone you haven't forgotten the items in the drawings in Activity 7 on the **Que sais-je?** page 348?
Can you see someone off?	How would you tell when these people are leaving, using the verb **partir?** 1. Didier / 14h28 2. Désirée et Annie / 20h46 3. Nous / 11h15 4. Tu / 23h59 How would you wish someone a good trip?

CHAPITRE 11

For an online self-test, go to go.hrw.com.

WA3 ARLES-11

Nom________________ Classe__________ Date__________

Vive les vacances!

TROISIEME ETAPE Student Make-Up Assignments Checklist

Pupil's Edition, pp. 337–339

Study the expressions in the **Comment dit-on... ?** box on page 337: asking for and expressing opinions. You should know how to ask someone's opinion and express yours.

- ☐ Do Activity 30, p. 337 as a writing activity. Rewrite the sentences to form a conversation.
- ☐ Do Activity 31, p. 338.
- ☐ Do Activity 32, p. 338 as a writing activity.
- ☐ Do Activity 33, p. 339.
- ☐ For additional practice, do Activities 17–19, pp. 128–129 in the **Cahier d'activités.**
- ☐ For additional practice, do Activity 4, CD 3 in the **Interactive CD-ROM Tutor.**

Nom ______________________ Classe ______________ Date ______________

TROISIEME ETAPE Self-Test

Can you ask for and express opinions?	How would you ask a friend how his or her vacation went? How would you tell how your vacation went?
Can you inquire about and relate past events?	How would you find out what a friend did on vacation? How would you tell what you did on vacation?

CHAPITRE 11

For an online self-test, go to **go.hrw.com**.

WA3 ARLES-11

Nom_______________ Classe_______________ Date_______________

CHAPITRE 12

En ville

PREMIERE ETAPE Student Make-Up Assignments Checklist

Pupil's Edition, pp. 359–362

Study the **Vocabulaire** on page 359.	☐ Do Activity 8, p. 360. ☐ Do Activity 9, p. 360 as a writing activity. Write complete sentences. ☐ Do Activity 10, p. 361 as a writing activity. ☐ Do Activity 11, p. 361 as a writing activity. ☐ For additional practice, do Activities 2–5, pp. 134–135 in the **Cahier d'activités.** ☐ For additional practice, do Activities 1–4, pp. 98–99 in the **Travaux pratiques de grammaire.** ☐ For additional practice, do Activities 1–2, CD 3 in the **Interactive CD-ROM Tutor.**
Study the expressions in the **Comment dit-on... ?** box on page 361: pointing out places and things. You should know how to point out places and things.	☐ Do Activity 12, p. 362 as a writing activity. ☐ Do Activity 13, p. 362. ☐ Do Activity 14, p. 362 as a writing activity. Write a conversation based on the clues from the activity. ☐ For additional practice, do Activity 8, p. 136 in the **Cahier d'activités.**

CHAPITRE 12

Nom ______________________ Classe ______________ Date ______________

PREMIERE ETAPE Self-Test

Can you point out places and things?	How would you point out and identify . . . 1. a certain building? 2. a certain store? 3. a certain person?

For an online self-test, go to **go.hrw.com**.

WA3 FORT-DE-FRANCE-12

CHAPITRE 12

Nom_______________ Classe_______________ Date_______________

En ville

DEUXIEME ETAPE Student Make-Up Assignments Checklist

Pupil's Edition, pp. 364–367

Study the expressions in the **Comment dit-on... ?** box on page 364: making and responding to requests. You should know how to make, accept, and decline requests.	☐ Do Activity 16, p. 365 as a writing activity. ☐ Do Activity 17, p. 365 as a writing activity. Write a conversation based on the clues in the activity. ☐ Do Activity 18, p. 365 as a writing activity. Write a conversation based on the clues in the activity. ☐ For additional practice, do Activities 9–11, p. 137 in the **Cahier d'activités.**
Study the expressions in the **Comment dit-on... ?** box on page 366: asking for advice and making suggestions. You should know how to ask for advice on how to get somewhere and suggest how to get somewhere.	☐ Do Activity 20, p. 367 as a writing activity. Write complete sentences.
Study the **Vocabulaire** on page 366.	☐ Do Activity 20, p. 367 as a writing activity. ☐ For additional practice, do Activities 12–14, p. 138 in the **Cahier d'activités.** ☐ For additional practice, do Activities 11–15, pp. 103–104 in the **Travaux pratiques de grammaire.** ☐ For additional practice, do Activity 4, CD 3 in the **Interactive CD-ROM Tutor.**
Study the grammar presentation in the **Grammaire** box on page 367: the pronoun **y.**	☐ Do Activity 21, p. 367 as a writing activity. ☐ Do Activity 22, p. 367 as a writing activity. Write a conversation based on the clues from the activity. ☐ For additional practice, do Activities 6–8, p. 378 in the **Grammaire supplémentaire.** ☐ For additional practice, do Activities 15–16, p. 139 in the **Cahier d'activités.**

- ☐ For additional practice, do Activities 16–17, p. 105 in the **Travaux pratiques de grammaire.**
- ☐ For additional practice, do Activity 5, CD 3 in the **Interactive CD-ROM Tutor.**

DEUXIEME ETAPE Self-Test

Can you make and respond to requests?	How would you ask someone to . . . 1. buy some stamps? 2. go to the bookstore? 3. deposit some money? How would you agree to do the favors you asked in the previous activity? How would you refuse?
Can you ask for advice and make suggestions?	How would you ask a friend which means of transportation you should use to get to a certain store? How would you suggest the means of transportation in the drawings in Activity 5 on the **Que sais-je?** page 382?

For an online self-test, go to **go.hrw.com**.

WA3 FORT-DE-FRANCE-12

Nom ______________ Classe ______________ Date ______________

En ville

TROISIEME ETAPE Student Make-Up Assignments Checklist

Pupil's Edition, pp. 369–373

Study the **Vocabulaire** on page 369.	☐ For additional practice, do Activities 18–20, p. 140 in the **Cahier d'activités.** ☐ For additional practice, do Activities 19–21, pp. 106–107 in the **Travaux pratiques de grammaire.**
Study the grammar presentation in the **Note de grammaire** box on page 369: the preposition **de.**	☐ Do Activity 25, p. 370 as a writing activity. ☐ Do Activity 26, p. 370. ☐ For additional practice, do Activities 9–10, p. 379 in the **Grammaire supplémentaire.** ☐ For additional practice, do Activity 21, p. 141 in the **Cahier d'activités.** ☐ For additional practice, do Activity 18, p. 106 in the **Travaux pratiques de grammaire.**
Study the expressions in the **Comment dit-on... ?** box on page 371: asking for and giving directions. You should know how to ask for and give directions.	☐ Do Activity 28, p. 371 as a writing activity. ☐ Do Activity 30, p. 373 as a writing activity. ☐ For additional practice, do Activities 22–24, pp. 141–142 in the **Cahier d'activités.** ☐ For additional practice, do Activity 6, CD 3 in the **Interactive CD-ROM Tutor.**

TROISIEME ETAPE Self-Test

Can you ask for and give directions?	How would you tell someone that you're looking for a certain place? How would you ask someone where a certain place in town is? How would you give someone directions to your house from . . . 1. your school? 2. your favorite restaurant?

For an online self-test, go to **go.hrw.com**.

WA3 FORT-DE-FRANCE-12

Alternative Quizzes

Nom ______________________ Classe ______________ Date ______________

CHAPITRE 1

Faisons connaissance!

Alternative Quiz 1-1A 

Maximum Score: 35/100

PREMIERE ETAPE

Grammar and Vocabulary

A. Circle the expression in each series that doesn't belong because of its meaning. (5 points)

1. très bien
   pas terrible
   comme ci comme ça
2. pas terrible
   très bien
   super
3. bof
   salut
   bonjour
4. au revoir
   tchao
   très bien
5. à bientôt
   à demain
   comme ci comme ça

SCORE ______

B. Read the conversation between Stéphanie and Valérie and figure out the words that were left out. Write the correct words in the blanks. (5 points)

Salut | Et toi | il s'appelle | Ça va | A tout à l'heure | Pas mal

Stéphanie (1) ______________, Valérie. Ça va?

Valérie (2) ______________. (3) ______________?

Stéphanie Bof! Dis, ton professeur, (4) ______________ comment?

Valérie Il s'appelle Frédéric Lemaire.

Stéphanie Bon. (5) ______________.

Valérie Au revoir.

SCORE ______

C. How would you say hello to these people in French? (5 points)

1. Your new friend's mother ______________
2. Your cousin Chris who is as old as you are ______________
3. Your five-year old neighbor ______________
4. Your best friend ______________
5. Your neighbor's grandfather ______________

SCORE ______

Alternative Quiz 1-1A

D. You've just met the new French exchange student, Camille. Respond in French to each of her statements and questions, using a complete sentence. (10 points)

1. Bonjour.

____

2. Comment ça va?

____

3. Tu t'appelles comment?

____

4. Tu as quel âge?

____

5. Au revoir.

____

SCORE

E. Write out the words in French for these numbers. (10 points)

1. twenty: ____________	6. eight: ____________
2. two: ____________	7. seventeen: ____________
3. fifteen: ____________	8. twelve: ____________
4. fourteen: ____________	9. nineteen: ____________
5. ten: ____________	10. thirteen: ____________

SCORE

TOTAL SCORE /35

Nom ______________________ Classe ______________ Date ______________

Faisons connaissance!

Alternative Quiz 1-2A 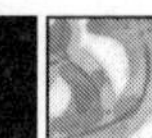

DEUXIEME ETAPE

Maximum Score: 30/100

Grammar and Vocabulary

A. Fill in the blanks with the appropriate definite articles. (6 points)

1. __________ ski
2. __________ hamburger
3. __________ pizza
4. __________ examen
5. __________ vélo
6. __________ frites

SCORE

B. Mark wants to write to his French pen pal about his interests, but he can't remember all the words he needs. Help him out by filling in the blanks in the sentences below with the words and phrases indicated. (6 points)

1. J'aime ____________________ *(French fries)*, mais je ____________________ *(don't like)* les hamburgers.
2. ____________________ *(I really like)* le cinéma, mais ____________________ *(I prefer)* les concerts.
3. J'aime ____________________ *(school)*.
4. J'adore ____________________ *(French)*.

SCORE

C. Céline is being difficult and answers in the negative to everything you ask her. Write her responses using complete sentences. (8 points)

1. Tu aimes la glace?

   ____

2. Tu aimes la plage?

   ____

Alternative Quiz 1-2A

3. Tu aimes le sport?

______

4. Tu aimes les vacances?

______

SCORE

D. Based on the information below, complete, in English, the report which summarizes the results of a recent survey of your classmates' interests. (10 points)

	n'aime pas	aime	aime mieux	adore
Stéphanie	le sport	l'école	le cinéma	les maths
Claude	le cinéma	la glace	le football	la plage
Eric	la plage	les escargots	les concerts	le football
Corinne	l'anglais	le chocolat	le français	les vacances

1. The two things that Claude likes the most are ______ and ______.
2. Stéphanie likes ______ the most.
3. Eric prefers ______ to concerts.
4. Claude prefers ice cream to ______.
5. Eric likes ______ the least.
6. Stéphanie prefers school to ______.
7. The two things that Corinne likes the least are ______ and ______.
8. Corinne likes ______ the most.

SCORE

TOTAL SCORE /30

CHAPITRE 1

Nom ______________________ Classe ______________ Date ______________

Faisons connaissance!

Alternative Quiz 1-3A 

TROISIEME ETAPE

Maximum Score: 35/100

Grammar and Vocabulary

A. Write in French the activity that is associated with these things. (7 points)

1. passport, ticket, suitcases ______________________
2. cassettes, CDs, boom box ______________________
3. mall, bags, credit card ______________________
4. books, magazines, newspaper ______________________
5. horses, saddle, fields ______________________
6. baseball bat, tennis shoes, hockey stick ______________________
7. ballet, tutu, music ______________________

SCORE ______

B. Answer these questions about what your friends like to do. Replace the underlined subjects with the correct subject pronoun. (8 points)

1. Delphine et Daniel aiment faire les magasins?

____

2. Karine et Christelle aiment faire du sport?

____

3. Est-ce que Jérôme adore regarder la télé?

____

4. Aurélie aime lire?

____

SCORE ______

C. Complete each of the following sentences with the correct form of the verb in parentheses. (10 points)

1. Vous ________ (étudier) le français?
2. Nous ________ (écouter) de la musique rock.
3. Paul et Marc ________ (danser) bien.

Alternative Quiz 1-3A

4. Chantal _________ (adore) nager.
5. Francine et Lise ________ (voyager) beaucoup.

SCORE

C. Read the letter that Elisa's pen pal wrote to her, and then answer, in English, the questions that follow. (10 points)

Chère Elisa,

Salut! Comment ça va? Qu'est-ce que tu aimes faire après l'école? Moi, j'aime écouter de la musique, mais je préfère sortir avec les copains. J'adore faire du sport. J'aime faire de l'équitation, mais j'aime surtout nager. J'aime bien les vacances parce que j'aime voyager.

A bientôt,

Bertrand

1. What does Bertrand like to do after school?

____

2. What does Bertrand like to do besides sports?

____

3. What sports does Bertrand like?

____

4. Does Bertrand mention any activities he does not like to do? If so, which one(s)?

____

5. Why does Bertrand like vacations?

____

SCORE

TOTAL SCORE /35

Nom ______________________ Classe ______________ Date ______________

Vive l'école!

Alternative Quiz 2-1A

PREMIERE ETAPE

Maximum Score: 30/100

Grammar and Vocabulary

A. Circle the subject that doesn't belong in each category. (5 points)

1. l'espagnol
   la chorale
   l'anglais
   le latin

2. le football
   la physique
   le volley
   le basket

3. l'histoire
   la géométrie
   l'algèbre
   les mathématiques

4. la musique
   la danse
   les arts plastiques
   la géographie

5. l'allemand
   la physique
   la chimie
   la biologie

SCORE [ ]

B. Tell what class you associate with each of the following people and things. (10 points)

la chimie la danse l'espagnol le français l'histoire le latin
l'informatique la géométrie le sport l'algèbre

1. Je m'appelle Julie ______________
2. FORTRAN ______________
3. Carré ______________
4. Napoléon Bonaparte ______________
5. 3x - y = 18 ______________
6. CO_2 ______________
7. Señor Martinez ______________
8. Modern ballet ______________
9. E pluribus unum ______________
10. Basket-ball ______________

SCORE [ ]

CHAPITRE 2

Nom ______________________ Classe ______________ Date ______________

Alternative Quiz 2-1A

C. You and your friend Marie-Claude are talking about your likes and dislikes. Using the expressions from the box below write an appropriate response to each of her questions and comments. Use each expression only once. (5 points)

Pas moi. | Moi, si. | Moi non plus. | Moi aussi. | Non, pas trop.

1. Tu n'aimes pas la pizza? ______________
2. Moi, j'adore le latin, et toi? ______________
3. Je n'aime pas les arts plastiques. ______________
4. J'adore la danse. ______________
5. Tu aimes la chimie? ______________

SCORE ______

D. Answer affirmatively to each of the following questions. Use a full sentence. (10 points)

1. Tu aimes l'espagnol?

____

2. Joël et Lise, vous n'aimez pas les sciences naturelles?

____

3. Elles n'aiment pas les examens?

____

4. Julien n'aime pas le latin?

____

5. Les élèves aiment le prof?

____

SCORE ______

TOTAL SCORE ______ /30

CHAPITRE 2

CHAPITRE 2

Nom ______________________ Classe ______________ Date ______________

Vive l'école!

Alternative Quiz 2-2A 

DEUXIEME ETAPE

Maximum Score: 35/100

Grammar and Vocabulary

A. At what times does each of the buses leave? Write out the times in French. (4 points)

1.	Nantes	11:00	______________________
2.	Montpellier	5:15	______________________
3.	Lille	16:25	______________________
4.	Lyon	18:45	______________________

SCORE

B. Look at the calendar and write which day of the week each date would be. (7 points)

SEPTEMBRE

L	M	M	J	V	S	D
		1	2	3	4	5
6	7	8	9	10	11	12
13	14	15	16	17	18	19
20	21	22	23	24	25	26
27	28	29	30			

1. le quatre ______________
2. le vingt-huit ______________
3. le dix ______________
4. le vingt-sept ______________
5. le cinq ______________
6. le vingt-neuf ______________
7. le vingt-trois ______________

SCORE

C. Marion and Serge are discussing their class schedule. Fill in the missing parts of their conversation, choosing from the box below. (4 points)

vous avez   nous avons   quels cours   j'ai

MARION Tu as (1) ______________ l'après-midi?

SERGE (2) ______________ histoire et anglais. Et, toi et Paul,

(3) ______________ latin?

MARION Oui, (4) ______________ latin avec Madame Lemaire.

SERGE Bon, à demain en cours de latin!

MARION Au revoir.

Nom ______________________ Classe ______________ Date ______________

Alternative Quiz 2-2A

D. Match these French words with their English equivalents. (8 points)

_____ 1. le déjeuner
_____ 2. le matin
_____ 3. aujourd'hui
_____ 4. l'après-midi
_____ 5. la récréation
_____ 6. maintenant
_____ 7. la sortie
_____ 8. l'étude

a. today
b. now
c. dismissal
d. morning
e. tomorrow
f. lunch
g. study hall
h. afternoon
i. break

SCORE

E. Write out the number of the buses you'd need to take to go to the various places listed. (6 points)

1.	32 Lyon	______________________
2.	59 Paris	______________________
3.	27 Tours	______________________
4.	53 Lourdes	______________________
5.	45 Poitiers	______________________
6.	41 Grenoble	______________________

SCORE

CHAPITRE 2

F. Complete each sentence using the correct form of **avoir**. (6 points)

1. Le lundi, Luc __________ espagnol.
2. Cet après-midi, tu __________ chimie.
3. Vous __________ arts plastiques demain à 14h00.
4. Ils __________ latin le mercredi et le vendredi?
5. Nous __________ sciences nat le matin?
6. J' __________ allemand maintenant.

SCORE

TOTAL SCORE /35

Nom _______________ Classe _______________ Date _______________

Vive l'école!

Alternative Quiz 2-3A 

TROISIEME ETAPE

Maximum Score: 35/100

Grammar and Vocabulary

A. Circle the item that does not belong with the others because of its meaning. (10 points)

1. bof
   comme ci comme ça
   cool
   pas mal

2. génial
   zéro
   intéressant
   passionnant

3. cool
   super
   difficile
   génial

4. difficile
   pas terrible
   pas génial
   nul

5. facile
   nul
   zéro
   barbant

SCORE

B. Place the words and expressions listed below in the appropriate categories. Use each word once. (15 points)

facile, bof, intéressant, passionnant, super, pas super, comme ci comme ça, pas génial, nul, zéro, pas mal, génial, barbant, cool, pas terrible

To express an unfavorable opinion	To express indifference	To express a favorable opinion

SCORE

Alternative Quiz 2-3A

C. Tell whether these students like **(L)** or dislike **(D)** their classes. (6 points)

1. C'est génial, les maths! _______
2. C'est nul, la chorale! _______
3. C'est passionnant, la géographie! _______
4. La biologie, c'est très intéressant! _______
5. C'est barbant, le français! _______
6. La chimie, c'est super! _______

SCORE [ ]

D. Tell what each of these students might say about the class in which he or she received this grade. Remember the French system is based on a scale of 0-20. (4 points)

_______	1. Lucien	8/20	**a.** C'est difficile!	**b.** C'est facile!
_______	2. Marie-Laure	17/20	**a.** C'est pas terrible!	**b.** C'est génial!
_______	3. Odile	10/20	**a.** C'est barbant!	**b.** C'est passionnant!
_______	4. Jean-Marie	18/20	**a.** C'est zéro!	**b.** C'est super!

SCORE [ ]

TOTAL SCORE [/35]

CHAPITRE

Nom_______________ Classe_______________ Date_______________

Tout pour la rentrée

Alternative Quiz 3-1A 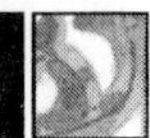

PREMIERE ETAPE

Maximum Score: 35/100

Grammar and Vocabulary

A. Complete the conversation between Lucien and Marcel with the appropriate indefinite articles. (10 points)

LUCIEN Marcel, qu'est-ce que tu as dans ton sac?

MARCEL Ben... j'ai **(1)** __________ trousse, **(2)** __________ crayons, **(3)** __________ classeur, **(4)** __________ cahiers et **(5)** __________ calculatrice, mais je n'ai pas **(6)** __________ stylo. Et toi?

LUCIEN Moi, j'ai **(7)** __________ gomme et **(8)** __________ stylos, mais je n'ai pas **(9)** __________ livre. Ah! J'ai aussi **(10)** __________ règle.

SCORE

B. Your French host mother has volunteered to shop for school supplies for you and three of your friends. Since her English is not very good, you're helping her translate all the lists into French. (10 points)

You:
an eraser
a pencil sharpener
a backpack

____
____
____

Jacob:
a pencil case
a loose-leaf binder

____
____
____

Alain:
a notebook
a calculator
a ruler

____
____
____

Renato:
sheets of paper
a book

____
____
____

SCORE

CHAPITRE 3

Nom ______________________ Classe ____________ Date ____________

Alternative Quiz 3-1A

C. What items would you need to do each of these tasks? Use each item only once. (5 points)

des règles — des trousses — des classeurs — des gommes — des livres — des calculatrices — des stylos

1. to read ______________________
2. to organize your class notes ______________________
3. to add a column of numbers ______________________
4. to hold pens and pencils ______________________
5. to draw a triangle in geometry class ______________________

SCORE ☐

D. You've forgotten to bring a lot of things to school today. Unfortunately, none of your friends has the supplies you need. Write their responses to your questions using complete sentences. (10 points)

1. Pauline, tu as une calculatrice?

____

2. Bertrand, tu as des feuilles de papier?

____

3. Raoul et Marie, vous avez des cahiers?

____

4. Jean-Claude, tu as un stylo?

____

5. Isabelle et Nathalie, vous avez des crayons?

____

SCORE ☐

TOTAL SCORE ☐ /35

Nom ________________ Classe ________________ Date ________________

CHAPITRE 3

Tout pour la rentrée

Alternative Quiz 3-2A 

DEUXIEME ETAPE

Maximum Score: 30/100

Grammar and Vocabulary

A. Complete the following sentences, choosing from the words in the box. (6 points)

un jean | des baskets | un magazine | une télévision | une radio | un ordinateur | un poster | une vidéocassette

1. Je voudrais acheter ________________ pour faire du sport.
2. Je voudrais acheter ________________ pour faire mes devoirs.
3. Je voudrais acheter ________________ pour regarder Monday Night Football®.
4. J'adore lire! Je voudrais acheter ________________.
5. Il me faut ________________ de Paris pour ma chambre *(room).*
6. Je voudrais acheter ________________ pour écouter de la musique.

SCORE ____

B. Marina and Chloé are shopping at a department store. Complete their conversation with the appropriate demonstrative adjectives. (7 points)

MARINA: Regarde Chloé, **(1)** ________________ montre, elle est super, non?

CHLOE: Oui, mais je préfère **(2)** ________________ montre-là.

MARINA: Qu'est-ce qu'il te faut pour l'école?

CHLOE: Il me faut **(3)** ________________ tee-shirt, **(4)** ________________ baskets et **(5)** ________________ short pour le sport. Et toi?

MARINA: Il me faut **(6)** ________________ cahier et **(7)** ________________ dictionnaire pour le français.

SCORE ____

CHAPITRE 3

Nom ______________________ Classe ______________ Date ______________

Alternative Quiz 3-2A

C. Your friend is trying to order some school supplies from a French store catalog on the Internet. Since his French is not as good as yours, help him out by completing the order list for him. Be sure to make the colors agree with the nouns they're describing. (14 points)

Il me faut des tee-shirts **(1)** ________________ *(white)*, une montre **(2)** ________________ *(purple)*, des stylos **(3)** ________________ *(black)*, une trousse **(4)** ________________ *(blue)*, des baskets **(5)** ________________ *(gray)*, deux cahiers **(6)** ________________ *(red)* et des crayons **(7)** ________________ *(green)*.

SCORE ______

D. Match these French words with their English equivalents. (3 points)

_____ **1.** des disques compacts

_____ **2.** des cassettes

_____ **3.** des montres

_____ **4.** des romans

_____ **5.** des ordinateurs

_____ **6.** des dictionnaires

a. CDs

b. novels

c. posters

d. sneakers

e. dictionaries

f. computers

g. cassette tapes

h. wallets

i. watches

SCORE ______

TOTAL SCORE ______ /30

CHAPITRE 3

CHAPITRE 3

Nom ______________________ Classe ______________ Date ______________

Tout pour la rentrée

Alternative Quiz 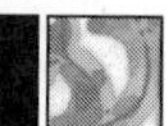

TROISIEME ETAPE

Maximum Score: 35/100

Grammar and Vocabulary

A. Write out these numbers in French. (20 points)

1. 601 ______________________
2. 279 ______________________
3. 999 ______________________
4. 373 ______________________
5. 385 ______________________
6. 500 ______________________
7. 617 ______________________
8. 267 ______________________
9. 794 ______________________
10. 93 ______________________

SCORE

B. Complete the conversation between Valérie and the salesperson using the appropriate expressions. (5 points)

C'est | Merci | C'est combien | A votre service | Excusez-moi | Comment tu trouves

VALERIE: (1) ______________________, madame.

(2) ______________________, ce classeur-là?

SALESPERSON: (3) ______________________ deux euros.

VALERIE: (4) ______________________, madame.

SALESPERSON: (5) ______________________.

SCORE

CHAPITRE 3

Nom ______________________ Classe ______________ Date ______________

Alternative Quiz 3-3A

C. Enter the correct price on each of these price tags. (10 points)

1. ______ soixante-quinze
2. ______ cent quatre-vingts
3. ______ quatre cent soixante-dix-huit
4. ______ soixante-quatorze
5. ______ neuf cent quarante-deux
6. ______ neuf cent cinquante-deux
7. ______ huit cent quatre-vingt-dix
8. ______ deux cent quarante-six
9. ______ quatre-vingt-huit
10. ______ cinq cent vingt-neuf

SCORE ______

TOTAL SCORE ______ /35

CHAPITRE 4

Nom ______________________ Classe ______________ Date ______________

Sports et passe-temps

CHAPITRE 4

Alternative Quiz 4-1A 

PREMIERE ETAPE

Maximum Score: 35/100

Grammar and Vocabulary

A. Group the following activities according to the categories below. (10 points)

faire du jogging, jouer au golf, faire du ski nautique, faire de la natation, jouer au football, faire de l'athlétisme, faire du roller en ligne, faire du vélo, jouer au volley, jouer au hockey

INDIVIDUAL SPORTS	TEAM SPORTS	WATER ACTIVITIES
______	______	______
______	______	______
______	______	______
______	______	______
______	______	______
______	______	______
______	______	______

SCORE ______

B. Match these activities with the appropriate English equivalent. (5 points)

_____ 1. jouer à des jeux vidéo

_____ 2. jouer aux cartes

_____ 3. faire du théâtre

_____ 4. faire de l'aérobic

_____ 5. regarder la télé

a. to play cards
b. to do aerobics
c. to watch tv
d. to play video games
e. to play soccer
f. to do drama
g. to do track and field

SCORE ______

Nom _______________ Classe _______________ Date _______________

Alternative Quiz 4-1A

C. Fill in the missing words to complete the descriptions of the sports and activities these people like and dislike. (10 points)

1. Pauline et Guy aiment ______________________ de la photo.
2. Je n'aime pas faire ______________________ ski.
3. Tu aimes ______________________ de la photo?
4. Nous adorons ______________________ au tennis.
5. Nicole aime jouer ______________________ base-ball.
6. J'aime faire ______________________ natation.
7. Elles aiment ______________________ du patin à glace.
8. Nous n'aimons pas ______________________ de la vidéo.
9. Tu aimes jouer ______________________ football américain?
10. Vous aimez faire ______________________ ski nautique?

SCORE ______

D. Magali interviewed several people about the sports and activities they or their friends like. Use **est-ce que** to recreate the questions she asked, based on the answers the people gave. (10 points)

1. MAGALI ______________________

   MARTIN Paul et moi? Oui, nous adorons faire du ski.

2. MAGALI ______________________

   BILL Charles et Gilles? Oui, ils adorent nager.

3. MAGALI ______________________

   SYLVIE Pierre? Non, il n'aime pas jouer aux cartes. Il préfère jouer au hockey.

4. MAGALI ______________________

   MAMADOU Oui, j'aime faire du vélo.

5. MAGALI ______________________

   SIMONE Onélia? Oui, elle aime bien lire.

SCORE ______

TOTAL SCORE ______ /35

Nom ______________________ Classe ______________ Date ______________

Sports et passe-temps

Alternative Quiz 4-2A

DEUXIEME ETAPE

Maximum Score: 35/100

Grammar and Vocabulary

A. Jean and Virginie are talking about activities they and their friends like to do. Fill in the blanks in the conversation below, with the correct forms of the verb **faire.** (8 points)

JEAN Mes amis et moi, nous adorons le sport. Et ton ami Louis, il **(1)** ______________ du sport?

VIRGINIE Non, Louis n'aime pas le sport. Est-ce que Pascale et toi, vous **(2)** ______________ du ski le week-end?

JEAN Non, le week-end, Pascale et moi, nous **(3)** ______________ du vélo. Le lundi et le mercredi, je **(4)** ______________ du patin à glace. Pascale et Sylvie **(5)** ______________ du jogging. Et toi? Tu **(6)** ______________ du sport en été?

VIRGINIE En été, je **(7)** ______________ souvent de la natation et Marie aime **(8)** ______________ du ski nautique.

SCORE

B. Frédéric wants to know about the sports and activities that Americans do. Answer his questions below. (4 points)

1. On joue au football américain en mai?

____

2. On joue au base-ball en décembre?

____

3. On fait du ski nautique au Canada en hiver?

____

4. On fait du ski en Floride au printemps?

____

SCORE

Nom ______________________ Classe ______________ Date ______________

CHAPITRE 4

Alternative Quiz 4-2A

C. Complete the following snippets of conversation by filling in the missing words and phrases. (10 points)

1. — Qu'est-ce que tu aimes faire quand ________________ *(it's hot)?*

2. — Quand ________________ *(it's raining)* en été, j'aime jouer aux cartes et regarder la télé.

3. — Et en hiver?

   — Quand ________________ *(it's cold),* j'aime faire du ski et du patin à glace.

4. — Qu'est-ce que tu aimes faire quand ________________ *(it's snowing)?*

   — J'aime lire ou faire de l'aérobic.

5. — Quand ________________ *(it's nice weather),* j'aime jouer au golf.

SCORE

D. Match the letter of the word that best fits each phrase. (5 points)

_____ 1. de dix-neuf heures à vingt-trois heures

_____ 2. de lundi à vendredi

_____ 3. octobre et novembre

_____ 4. mars et avril

_____ 5. juin et juillet

a. l'été
b. le printemps
c. l'hiver
d. le soir
e. l'automne
f. la semaine

SCORE

E. Create complete sentences out of the words below by conjugating the verbs and making any other necessary changes. (8 points)

1. ils / aimer / jouer / base-ball

   ____

2. est-ce que / elle / parler / français

   ____

3. je / ne... pas / jouer / volley

   ____

4. nous / aimer / faire / roller en ligne

   ____

SCORE

TOTAL SCORE /35

Nom ______________________ Classe ______________ Date ______________

Sports et passe-temps

Alternative Quiz 4-3A 

TROISIEME ETAPE

Maximum Score: 30/100

Grammar and Vocabulary

A. Read what these students say about the sports they like, and then indicate whether the statements that follow are **vrai** (true) or **faux** (false). (6 points)

KOFFI J'adore faire du sport. Je joue au foot trois ou quatre fois par semaine. Le lundi, le mercredi et le samedi soir, je fais du jogging. D'habitude, je joue au basket le mardi et le dimanche. De temps en temps, je fais du vélo.

CHANTAL Moi, j'aime bien le sport. Quelquefois, je fais du roller ou de l'aérobic. Je fais souvent du vélo. Je ne fais jamais de jogging.

AHMED Je n'aime pas beaucoup le sport. D'habitude, je préfère regarder la télé ou écouter de la musique. Quelquefois, je fais du roller et je joue au foot une fois par semaine.

MARIE Le sport, c'est super! Je fais de l'aérobic trois fois par semaine. Le samedi soir, je fais du jogging. L'hiver, je fais souvent du patin à glace et du ski.

_______ 1. Chantal does aerobics more often than Marie.

_______ 2. Koffi plays soccer about as often as Ahmed does.

_______ 3. Chantal jogs sometimes.

_______ 4. Koffi rides his bike more often than Chantal does.

_______ 5. Chantal goes in-line skating about as often as Ahmed does.

_______ 6. Marie jogs more often than Koffi does.

SCORE

B. Unscramble and complete the fragments below to form logical sentences. Be sure to make any necessary changes. (12 points)

1. je / natation / de temps en temps / faire

____

2. athlétisme / faire / nous / une fois par semaine

____

3. vidéo / ne... jamais / vous / faire

____

4. tu / souvent / est-ce que / ski / faire

____

CHAPITRE 4

Alternative Quiz 4-3A

5. faire / Corinne et Nicole / photo / quelquefois

____

6. vélo / rarement / faire / ils

____

SCORE

C. Tell how often these students do the following activities, according to the calendars below. (12 points)

LUNDI	MARDI	MERCREDI	JEUDI	VENDREDI	SAMEDI	DIMANCHE
natation	vélo		vélo	natation		vélo
vélo		vélo	vélo	vélo		natation

1. Julien (vélo)

____

2. Julien (natation)

____

LUNDI	MARDI	MERCREDI	JEUDI	VENDREDI	SAMEDI	DIMANCHE
	ski					ski
					ski	

3. Odile (ski)

____

LUNDI	MARDI	MERCREDI	JEUDI	VENDREDI	SAMEDI	DIMANCHE
		patin à glace				

4. Patricia (patin à glace)

____

SCORE

TOTAL SCORE /30

Nom ______________________ Classe ______________ Date ______________

On va au café?

Alternative Quiz 5-1A 

PREMIERE ETAPE

Maximum Score: 30/100

Grammar and Vocabulary

A. Respond to your friend's suggestions according to the cues below. Use a different response each time. (8 points)

1. On va chez Pierre?

   (-) ____

2. On va au cinéma?

   (+) ____

3. On fait du vélo?

   (-) ____

4. Prends un hot-dog!

   (+) ____

SCORE ☐

B. Help Noëlle translate these words so she can create a menu for her school's National Foreign Language Week celebration. (8 points)

Les sandwiches:

1. ham sandwich ____
2. salami sandwich ____
3. toasted ham and cheese sandwich ______________________________
4. cheese sandwich ____

Les boissons:

1. lemon soda ____
2. water with strawberry syrop ______________________________
3. orange juice ____
4. cola ____

SCORE ☐

Nom ______________________ Classe ______________ Date ______________

Alternative Quiz 5-1A

C. Pierre and his friends are at a restaurant, and they're deciding what to get. Complete Pierre's explanation about what they usually eat. Use the correct forms of the verb **prendre.** (6 points)

On va au café après l'école pour **(1)** ______________ quelque chose. D'habitude, Lucien et Dominique **(2)** ______________ des croque-monsieur. Sylvie n'aime pas manger en général, mais parfois, elle **(3)** ______________ un hot-dog. Marcel et moi, nous **(4)** ______________ de la quiche, mais des fois, je **(5)** ______________ une salade. Et toi? Qu'est-ce que tu **(6)** ______________ au café?

SCORE ______

D. Make suggestions to the new exchange students about what to do based on their interests. (8 points)

1. Pierre likes to play video games.

____

2. Chantal likes to eat.

____

3. Michel likes to have coffee.

____

4. Sophie likes to swim.

____

CHAPITRE 5

SCORE ______

TOTAL SCORE ______ /30

Nom _______________ Classe _______________ Date _______________

On va au café?

Alternative Quiz 5-2A 

DEUXIEME ETAPE

Maximum Score: 35/100

Grammar and Vocabulary

A. Tell your friends what to do, using the cues provided in parentheses. (16 points)

1. Benoît (prendre des photos)

   ____

2. Armande et Thuy (donner les sandwiches aux élèves)

   ____

3. Luc (parler au professeur)

   ____

4. Dominique (faire les sandwiches)

   ____

5. Odile et Chantal (apporter les boissons)

   ____

6. Coralie et Marcel (faire attention)

   ____

7. Gustave et Julien (prendre des notes)

   ____

8. Aurélie (regarder le tableau)

   ____

SCORE ☐

B. What advice would you give these classmates? Give them a suggestion using the imperative form of a verb from the box below. Use each verb only once. (10 points)

faire	manger	écouter	prendre	jouer

1. — J'adore la musique.

   — _______________ la radio!

CHAPITRE 5

Alternative Quiz 5-2A

2. — Je ne suis pas fort en maths.
   — ______________________ tes devoirs!
3. — J'ai faim.
   — ______________________ un sandwich!
4. — J'aime le sport.
   — ______________________ au golf!
5. — J'ai soif.
   — ______________________ une limonade!

SCORE

C. You're putting together a French phrase book for American students. Categorize these phrases according to whether they would be used to get someone's attention or to order food and beverages. (9 points)

Je voudrais un coca. Mademoiselle! Excusez-moi. La carte, s'il vous plaît. Apportez-moi une crêpe. Monsieur! Donnez-moi une limonade. Je vais prendre un hot-dog. Madame!

TO GET SOMEONE'S ATTENTION

____

____

____

____

____

TO ORDER FOOD AND BEVERAGES

____

____

____

____

____

SCORE

TOTAL SCORE /35

CHAPITRE 5

CHAPITRE 5

Nom______________________ Classe______________ Date______________

On va au café?

Alternative Quiz 5-3A 

TROISIEME ETAPE

Maximum Score: 35/100

Grammar and Vocabulary

A. The Café des Etoiles lets you pay for your meal by check. Based on the totals shown below, what number would you have to write out on your check if you ordered these items? (20 points)

1. Deux sandwiches au fromage : 7 euros

____

2. Un croque-monsieur : 9 euros

____

3. Cinq coupes Melba : 11 euros

____

4. Une grande pizza : 16 euros

____

5. Un hamburger : 4,5 euros

____

6. Cinq cocas : 12 euros

____

7. Deux glaces : 8 euros

____

8. Cinq jus de fruit : 13 euros

____

9. Trois steaks-frites : 20 euros

____

10. Trois hot-dogs : 10 euros

____

SCORE [ ]

CHAPITRE 5

Nom ______________________ Classe ______________ Date ______________

Alternative Quiz 5-3A

B. Complete these conversations, using the phrases provided below. (8 points)

Vous avez **c'est combien** **l'addition, s'il vous plaît** **Oui, tout de suite** **Ça fait combien** **Ça fait**

1. — Le jus de pomme, ______________________?

   — C'est 2,50 euros, monsieur.

2. — ______________________?

   — Ça fait dix euros.

3. — Un steak-frites, s'il vous plaît.

   — ______________________, madame.

4. — Excusez-moi, monsieur, (4) ______________________.

   — Oui, voilà, madame.

SCORE ____

CHAPITRE 5

C. Which of these expressions will you hear if you overhear someone talking about a meal or someone trying to pay the bill? (7 points)

Ça fait combien, s'il vous plaît? **L'addition, s'il vous plaît..** **C'est dégoûtant.** **C'est super.** **C'est pas bon** **C'est délicieux.** **C'est combien pour le hot-dog et le coca?**

TO TALK ABOUT A MEAL	TO PAY FOR THE BILL
______________	______________
______________	______________
______________	______________
______________	______________

SCORE ____

TOTAL SCORE ____ /35

Nom _______________ Classe _______________ Date _______________

Amusons-nous!

Alternative Quiz 6-1A 

PREMIERE ETAPE

Maximum Score: 30/100

Grammar and Vocabulary

A. Tell your friends where to go based on their interests. (10 points)

1. Marie aime faire les magasins.

____

2. Pierre adore les films.

____

3. Damien aime la mer.

____

4. Karine et Joëlle adorent faire des pique-niques.

____

5. Alain et Renato aiment faire du jogging.

____

SCORE [ ]

B. Match these activities with the places you would go to do them. (5 points)

_____ 1. Je vais voir une exposition d'art moderne...	**a.** à la piscine
_____ 2. Je vais faire les magasins...	**b.** au parc
_____ 3. Je vais voir les animaux exotiques...	**c.** au centre commercial
_____ 4. Je vais chercher quelque chose à lire...	**d.** au zoo
_____ 5. Je vais nager...	**e.** à la bibliothèque
	f. au musée

SCORE [ ]

Nom ______________________ Classe ______________ Date ______________

Alternative Quiz 6-1A

C. Tell what your classmates are going to do this weekend by rearranging the cues in the correct order and writing complete sentences. Be sure to make all the necessary changes. (10 points)

1. pour le bac / aller / tu / étudier

   ____

2. au / faire un pique-nique / aller / nous / parc

   ____

3. avec / au téléphone / nous / parler / les copains / aller

   ____

4. patin à glace / Karine / faire /aller /du /dimanche

   ____

5. les / aller / samedi / Roger / magasins / faire

   ____

SCORE ____

D. Brigitte is talking about her plans for this weekend. Fill in the blanks with the appropriate forms of **aller.** (5 points)

D'habitude, mes amis et moi, nous **(1)** ______________ au centre commercial le samedi, mais ce samedi, c'est différent. Robin et Claude **(2)** ______________ faire un pique-nique au parc. André **(3)** ______________ aller au musée et moi, je **(4)** ______________ voir un film au cinéma. Et toi? Qu'est-ce que tu **(5)** ______________ faire ce week-end?

SCORE ____

TOTAL SCORE ____ /30

CHAPITRE 6

CHAPITRE 6

Nom _______________ Classe _______________ Date _______________

Amusons-nous!

Alternative Quiz 6-2A 

DEUXIEME ETAPE

Maximum Score: 30/100

Grammar and Vocabulary

A. You and your friends are making plans for the weekend. Tell what everyone wants to do by rearranging the cues and completing each sentence with the correct forms of **vouloir.** Make all the necessary changes. (12 points)

1. soir / nous / un film / vouloir / dimanche / voir

____

2. aller / et Laurent / vouloir / Sophie / piscine / à la

____

3. rester / je / chez moi / vouloir

____

4. vouloir / tu / un match / regarder / de football

____

5. Nathalie / zoo / vouloir / et moi / aller / nous / au

____

6. aller / Gigi / centre commercial / vouloir / au

____

SCORE

B. Complete each sentence with the correct subject pronoun from the box below. (5 points)

Vous	Je	Elle	Nous	Ils

1. _______________ veux voir une pièce de théâtre.
2. _______________ voulons aller à la plage.
3. _______________ veulent aller à une boum.
4. _______________ veut faire les magasins.
5. _______________ voulez regarder la télé?

SCORE

CHAPITRE 6

Nom ______________________ Classe ______________ Date ______________

Alternative Quiz 6-2A

C. Categorize the answers to invitations in the box below. Write down each phrase under the appropriate column title: Accept or Refuse. (8 points)

J'ai des trucs à faire. Bonne idée. Désolée, je suis occupée. Pourquoi pas? Ça ne me dit rien. Je veux bien. D'accord. Désolé, je ne peux pas.

ACCEPT	REFUSE
______________	______________
______________	______________
______________	______________
______________	______________

SCORE

D. Match the sentences below with the logical response. Use each response only once. (5 points)

_____ **1.** J'ai soif.

_____ **2.** J'adore Dalí!

_____ **3.** Tu ne viens pas?

_____ **4.** On peut faire du ski nautique.

_____ **5.** Je voudrais nager.

a. Allons à la plage!

b. Allons au musée!

c. Bonne idée. J'adore aller à la piscine.

d. Tu veux venir au café avec moi?

e. Non, j'ai des trucs à faire.

f. Moi, non plus.

SCORE

TOTAL SCORE /30

Nom ______________________ Classe ______________ Date ______________

Amusons-nous!

Alternative Quiz 6-3A 

TROISIEME ETAPE

Maximum Score: 40/100

Grammar and Vocabulary

A. Write out the times below in conversational French. Make sure you mention whether it's in the morning, in the afternoon, or in the evening. (12 points)

1. 2:20 P.M. ______________________
2. 11:10 A.M. ______________________
3. 6:40 P.M. ______________________
4. 7:55 A.M. ______________________
5. 8:50 A.M. ______________________
6. 6:15 A.M. ______________________

SCORE ______

B. Match the responses on the left with the appropriate question from the column on the right. (10 points)

______ 1. Il est quinze heures.	a. Quand?
______ 2. A six heures.	b. Avec qui?
______ 3. Demain matin.	c. Où ça?
______ 4. Avec mes copains.	d. A quelle heure?
______ 5. A midi.	e. Quelle heure est-il?
______ 6. Avec Sophie.	
______ 7. Chez ma tante.	
______ 8. Au parc St-Germain.	
______ 9. Il est trois heures et demie.	
______ 10. Ce week-end.	

SCORE ______

Nom ______________________ Classe ______________ Date ______________

Alternative Quiz 6-3A

C. Lætitia is talking on the phone with Sophie. You can only hear one side of their conversation. Using complete sentences, write what Sophie might logically be saying. (8 points)

LAETITIA Je veux aller à la plage. Tu viens?

SOPHIE (1) ______________________________

LAETITIA Avec Jacques et Claire.

SOPHIE (2) ______________________________

LAETITIA Dimanche matin.

SOPHIE (3) ______________________________

LAETITIA Chez moi.

SOPHIE (4) ______________________________

LAETITIA A neuf heures. On se retrouve vers 8h30.

SCORE ____

D. You're responsible for a group of French exchange students who've just arrived in your town. Ask them the following questions, so that you can stay informed of their whereabouts. (10 points)

1. What are you going to do at half past three this afternoon?

____

2. Where are you going on Tuesday at noon?

____

3. When are you going to the zoo?

____

4. At what time are we meeting?

____

5. With whom are you going to the swimming pool?

____

SCORE ____

TOTAL SCORE ____ /40

CHAPITRE 6

Nom _______________ Classe _______________ Date _______________

La famille

Alternative Quiz 7-1A

PREMIERE ETAPE

Maximum Score: 35/100

Grammar and Vocabulary

A. As you look through a family photo album, you come across several wedding photos. Explain to your little brother who everyone is. Complete the sentences with **du, de la, de l'**, or **des.** (5 points)

1. Ce sont les parents _______________ grands-parents de Martine.
2. C'est la mère _______________ cousin de Michel.
3. C'est l'oncle _______________ sœur de Mathieu.
4. C'est le fils _______________ oncle d'Odile.
5. C'est la sœur _______________ père de Guillaume.

SCORE

B. Complete each of the following sentences with the correct possessive adjective. (10 points)

1. Je cherche _______________ tee-shirts.
2. Bernard et Yves ont _______________ livre.
3. Céline a _______________ montre.
4. Nous aimons _______________ photos.
5. Tu cherches _______________ sœurs.
6. Marc a _______________ radio.
7. Nous avons _______________ baskets.
8. Tu aimes _______________ disques compacts.
9. Vous parlez avec _______________ grand-père.
10. Je cherche _______________ amie.

SCORE

Nom ______________________ Classe ______________ Date ______________

CHAPITRE 7

Alternative Quiz 7-1A

C. Which member of Joséphine's family is she talking about in the sentences below? Answer using **son, sa,** or **ses.** (20 points)

1. Voilà le frère de ma mère.
   ____
2. C'est le père de ma mère.
   ____
3. Voilà la mère de mon cousin.
   ____
4. Voici le mari de ma mère.
   ____
5. Voici la sœur de mon cousin.
   ____
6 C'est la mère de mon frère.
   ____
7. Voilà le frère de ma sœur.
   ____
8. C'est la mère de mon père.
   ____
9. C'est la femme de mon oncle.
   ____
10. Voici la sœur de ma mère.
   ____

SCORE ______

TOTAL SCORE ______ /35

Nom ______________________ Classe ______________ Date ______________

7 La famille

Alternative Quiz 7-2A 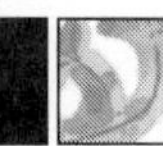

Maximum Score: 30/100

DEUXIEME ETAPE

Grammar and Vocabulary

A. For everything that Elodie describes, her sister, Elmire, makes a similar comparison. Complete Elmire's statements making all necessary changes to the adjectives. (8 points)

1. — Notre père est sympa.

   — Notre mère est ______________________ aussi.

2. — Nos cousins sont forts.

   — Nos cousines sont ______________________ aussi.

3. — Mon pull est blanc.

   — Mes montres sont ______________________ aussi.

4. — Notre oncle est grand.

   — Notre tante est ______________________ aussi.

5. — Notre frère est intéressant.

   — Nos cousins sont ______________________ aussi.

6. — Mon ami est gentil.

   — Mon amie est ______________________ aussi.

7. — Notre grand-père est âgé.

   — Nos grands-mères sont ______________________ aussi.

8. — Notre chien est timide.

   — Nos chats sont ______________________ aussi.

SCORE ☐

B. Chantal is describing her family to her friends as they look at a photo album. Fill in the missing words to complete her descriptions. (8 points)

— Voici mon père. Il est **(1)** ______________________ *(brown-headed)* et

(2) ______________________ *(fat)*. Il n'est **(3)** ______________________ *(medium height)*.

— Regardez mon frère. Il est **(4)** ______________________ *(nice)* et

(5) ______________________ *(short)*. Il n'est pas **(6)** ______________________ *(slender)*!

Alternative Quiz 7-2A

— Voici ma mère. Elle est **(7)** ______ *(smart)* et

(8) ______ *(redheaded)*.

SCORE

C. Use the correct forms of **être** to complete these sentences. (8 points)

1. Vous ne (n') ______ ni grands ni petits.
2. Tu ______ sympa.
3. Paul et Gilles ______ grands.
4. Odile ______ gentille.
5. Nous ne (n') ______ pas timides.
6. Je ______ intelligent.
7. Ils ne (n') ______ ni pénibles ni méchants.
8. Ma mère ______ super gentille.

SCORE

D. Rewrite these sentences using the underlined adjectives and making all the necessary changes. (6 points)

1. Voici un chien <u>méchant</u>.

   Voici des chats ______.
2. C'est un sport <u>passionnant</u>.

   Ce sont des films ______.
3. Je cherche un livre <u>amusant</u>.

   Je cherche des romans ______.
4. Tu as un cousin <u>roux</u>.

   Tu as des cousines ______.
5. Nous avons un cahier <u>orange</u>.

   Nous avons des baskets ______.
6. Tu as un <u>petit</u> frère.

   Tu as deux ______ cousines.

SCORE

TOTAL SCORE /30

Nom ______________ Classe ______________ Date ______________

La famille

Alternative Quiz 7-3A

TROISIEME ETAPE

Maximum Score: 35/100

Grammar and Vocabulary

A. Isabelle likes to do indoor activities, while Angèle enjoys outdoor activities. Write the name of an activity from the box under the name of the person who would like to do it. (8 points)

faire les courses | passer l'aspirateur | ranger les chambres | faire la vaisselle | promener le chien | tondre le gazon | laver la voiture | garder sa sœur

ISABELLE	ANGELE
______________	______________
______________	______________
______________	______________
______________	______________

SCORE ______

B. Unscramble the cues below and write logical, complete sentences. Make all the necessary changes. (12 points)

1. la vaisselle / aimer / Paul / faire / est-ce que
____
2. gentil / ne...pas / Martine / être
____
3. ta chambre / tu / ranger / le / samedi
____
4. ne...pas / débarrasser / aimer / mon cousin / la table
____
5. le gazon / mon père / chaque / et mon frère / tondre / week-end
____
6. ma / chien / quelquefois / et moi / le / promener / sœur / nous
____

SCORE ______

Alternative Quiz 7-3A

C. Put each of these sentences under the appropriate category. (8 points)

C'est impossible. Bien sûr! Pas question! Si tu veux.
D'accord. Pas ce soir. Tu es d'accord? Je peux sortir?

ASKING FOR PERMISSION	GIVING PERMISSION	REFUSING PERMISSION
______	______	______
______	______	______
______	______	______
______	______	______

SCORE ______

D. The French Club has volunteered for community service this weekend. Read the teacher's list of chores, and then answer the questions that follow. (7 points)

Antoinette doit sortir la poubelle.
Olivier doit passer l'aspirateur.
Fabien et Jérôme doivent tondre le gazon.
Julien doit débarrasser la table.
Martine doit faire la vaisselle.
Florent, Monique et Marc doivent ranger les chambres.
Et tout le monde doit faire le ménage.

1. Who gets to do the dishes? ______
2. What is everyone going to do? ______
3. Who is responsible for mowing the lawn? ______
4. Who is going to take out the trash? ______
5. What is Monique going to do? ______
6. Who gets to vacuum? ______
7. Who is in charge of cleaning the table? ______

SCORE ______

TOTAL SCORE ______ /35

Nom ______________________ Classe ______________ Date ______________

Au marché

Alternative Quiz 8-1A

PREMIERE ETAPE

Maximum Score: 35/100

Grammar and Vocabulary

A. Complete these conversations with the appropriate partitive or indefinite article. (10 points)

1. — Tu vas au marché?

   — Oui, qu'est-ce qu'il te faut?

   — Il me faut ________ pain pour le dîner. Et prends aussi ________ beurre. Je vais faire ________ tarte pour le dessert.

2. — Tu veux ________ confiture?

   — Oui. Est-ce qu'il y a ________ beurre?

   — Bien sûr. Et il y a ________ chocolat aussi.

3. — Je veux faire ________ salade de fruits. Tu peux prendre ________ bananes, ________ papayes et ________ citron au marché?

   — D'accord.

SCORE ______

B. Members of the French Club are going to buy food for a cultural project. Gabrielle will buy dairy and meat products, Agnès will get fruit, and Cédric will get vegetables. Write which food items each person is responsible for on their lists below. (15 points)

des fraises
des papayes
du maïs
des mangues
des pommes de terre
des haricots verts
du lait
des pêches
des goyaves
des yaourts
des ananas
du fromage
du porc
des champignons
du bœuf

Gabrielle	Agnès	Cédric
________	________	________
________	________	________
________	________	________
________	________	________
________	________	________
________	________	________
________	________	________

SCORE ______

Alternative Quiz 8-1A

C. Circle the item that doesn't belong in each set. (5 points)

1. le maïs
   le poisson
   le poulet
2. le beurre
   le fromage
   le riz
3. les oignons
   les fraises
   les pêches
4. l'eau minérale
   le jus de pomme
   le bœuf
5. les goyaves
   les champignons
   les gombos

SCORE

D. You're working as the chef's assistant at a famous French restaurant. Answer the chef's questions by circling the appropriate item. (5 points)

1. Qu'est-ce qu'il te faut pour faire un gâteau?
   a. de la farine **b.** du riz **c.** des haricots verts
2. De quoi est-ce que tu as besoin pour faire une salade de fruits?
   a. de viande **b.** de haricots verts **c.** de bananes
3. Qu'est-ce qu'il te faut pour faire une omelette?
   a. des fraises **b.** des œufs **c.** du riz
4. Qu'est-ce qu'il te faut pour faire des spaghettis?
   a. des poires **b.** des tomates **c.** des noix de coco
5. De quoi est-ce que tu as besoin pour faire un croque-monsieur?
   a. de poisson **b.** de maïs **c.** de jambon

SCORE

TOTAL SCORE /35

CHAPITRE 8

Nom _______________ Classe _______________ Date _______________

Au marché

Alternative Quiz 8-2A 

DEUXIEME ETAPE

Maximum Score: 30/100

Grammar and Vocabulary

A. Bertrand is going on vacation for a month, and some of his friends are volunteering to help with chores while he's gone. Use the correct form of **pouvoir** to complete their statements. (6 points)

1. Je _______________ sortir la poubelle.
2. Emilie et Samuel, vous _______________ garder le chat, et toi, Marc, tu _______________ promener le chien.
3. Isabelle _______________ laver la voiture.
4. Pierre et Jeanne _______________ aller à la poste.
5. Sylvie et moi, nous _______________ tondre le gazon.

SCORE [ ]

CHAPITRE 8

B. Rewrite these sentences using the quantities in parentheses. (12 points)

1. Achète-moi du porc! (two kilos)

____

2. Voici du jambon. (eight slices)

____

3. Donne-moi des pêches! (three cans)

_______________!

4. Je voudrais des oranges. (a dozen)

____

5. Tu me rapportes du riz? (a box)

____

6. Il me faut du gâteau. (a piece)

____

SCORE [ ]

Nom ______________________ Classe ______________ Date ______________

Alternative Quiz 8-2A

C. Complete these conversations by filling in the missing expressions. (12 points)

1. — ______________________ de ranger ta chambre!
   (Don't forget)

   — D'accord.

2. — On va au cinéma ce soir?

   — ______________________?
   (Why not)

3. — ______________________ du pain et du beurre, Laurent.
   (Buy me)

   — ______________________, Maman. J'y vais tout de suite.
   (Well, OK.)

4. — ______________________ faire la vaisselle?
   (Can you)

   — Je regrette, mais ______________________.
   (I can't right now.)

SCORE ______

TOTAL SCORE ______ /30

CHAPITRE 8

Nom______________________ Classe______________ Date______________

Au marché

Alternative Quiz 8-3A 

Maximum Score: 35/100

TROISIEME ETAPE

Grammar and Vocabulary

A. Match the following expressions with their English equivalents. (7 points)

_____	**1.** Vous voulez...	**a.**	I'm not hungry anymore.
_____	**2.** J'en veux bien...	**b.**	More...
_____	**3.** Encore...	**c.**	I'd like some...
_____	**4.** Je n'ai plus faim.	**d.**	Will you have...
_____	**5.** Vous prenez...	**e.**	With pleasure.
_____	**6.** Je n'en veux plus...	**f.**	I don't want anymore.
_____	**7.** Avec plaisir.	**g.**	Would you like...

SCORE

B. You're in charge of the kitchen at camp. Plan your meal schedule by writing the letter of the meal at which each menu is most likely to be served. (12 points)

a. le petit déjeuner **b. le déjeuner ou le dîner** **c. le goûter**

1. _____
des œufs
du jus d'orange
des céréales
du lait

2. _____
un sandwich au fromage
une salade
un yaourt
une pêche

3. _____
des gâteaux
un coca
du chocolat

4. _____
une salade
du pain
de l'eau minérale

5. _____
un café
de la confiture
du beurre
du pain

6. _____
du poisson
du riz
des haricots verts
des fraises

SCORE

Nom ______________________ Classe ______________ Date ______________

Alternative Quiz 8-3A

C. Use these cues to write complete sentences that might be overheard at a restaurant. Be sure to conjugate the verbs and add any necessary articles. (10 points)

1. nous / vouloir / sandwiches au fromage

____

2. je / ne... pas / prendre / gombos

____

3. vous / vouloir / eau minérale

____

4. tu / vouloir / viande

____

5. ils / prendre / fraises

____

SCORE

CHAPITRE 8

D. You're helping your parent decide what needs to be bought at the grocery store. Answer your parent's question according to the cues given. Use the pronoun **en** in your answers. (6 points)

1. — Nous avons des citrons?

   — Non, ____

2. — Nous avons des yaourts?

   — Oui, ____

3. — Nous avons du jus de pomme?

   — Oui, ____

4. — Nous avons des concombres?

   — Non, ____

5. — Nous avons des tomates?

   — Oui, ____

6. - Nous avons du poisson?

   - Non, ____

SCORE

TOTAL SCORE /35

Nom_______________ Classe_______________ Date_______________

Au téléphone

Alternative Quiz 9-1A 

PREMIERE ETAPE

Maximum Score: 30/100

Grammar and Vocabulary

A. Olivier is asking Corinne about her weekend. Use the **passé composé** of the verbs in parentheses to complete their conversation. (8 points)

OLIVIER Tu **(1)** _______________ (passer) un bon week-end?

CORINNE Oui, samedi Sophie et moi, nous **(2)** _______________ (aller) à la plage, et je/j' **(3)** _______________ (voir) quelques amis.

OLIVIER Qu'est-ce que vous **(4)** _______________ (faire)?

CORINNE Nous **(5)** _______________ (nager) et après nous **(6)** _______________ (manger) des sandwiches.

OLIVIER Et après ça?

CORINNE Je/J' **(7)** _______________ (prendre) le bus et je/j' **(8)** _______________ (retrouver) Lucie au cinéma.

SCORE

B. Complete each of these conversations logically with the **passé composé** of the verb in parentheses and the appropriate adverb from the box. Use each adverb only once. (10 points)

beaucoup	ne...pas encore	souvent	trop	déjà

1. — Pendant les vacances, Sarah est sortie le soir?

   — Oui, tous les soirs! Et elle _______________ (voir) des films au cinéma.

2. — Tu as vu le théâtre antique d'Arles?

   — Non, je/j' _______________ (visiter) les monuments d'Arles.

3. — Thérèse et Jean, vous voulez déjeuner à la cantine avec moi?

   — Non merci, nous _______________ (manger) chez nous.

Nom ______________________ Classe ______________ Date ______________

Alternative Quiz 9-1A

4. — Est-ce que ta sœur a voyagé, l'année dernière?

   — Oui! Elle ______________________ (voyager). Au Mexique, au Brésil et en Colombie.

5. — Qu'est-ce que Gérard a pris au fast-food?

   — Huit hamburgers avec des frites. Il ______________________ (manger)!

SCORE

C. Unscramble the cues provided to write complete sentences in the **passé composé.** Be sure to make any necessary changes. (12 points)

1. devoirs / tu / oublier / de / tes / géométrie

   ____?

2. sympa / au / fille / commercial / Marc / rencontrer / centre / une

   ____.

3. la / déjeuner / vous / cantine / jours / à / les / tous

   ____.

4. amis / et Sophie / au / des / retrouver / Justine / café

   ____.

5 gagner / et / je / je / fast-food / euros / travailler / au / cent vingt

   ____.

6. CD / nous / euros / cent / nous / acheter / parce que / quatre / trouver

   ____.

SCORE

TOTAL SCORE /30

CHAPITRE 9

Nom_______________ Classe_______________ Date_______________

Au téléphone

Alternative Quiz 9-2A

DEUXIEME ETAPE

Maximum Score: 35/100

Grammar and Vocabulary

A. Your computer has a virus and it has scrambled the script of a French play that you're directing. Put the following script of a telephone conversation in the most logical order by numbering the lines from 1 to 7. (7 points)

_____ **a.** — Vous pouvez lui dire qu'on va au stade à six heures et demie?

_____ **b.** — Allô?

_____ **c.** — Bonjour! C'est Sandrine Michot à l'appareil. Nicole est là, s'il vous plaît?

_____ **d.** — Oui. Mais, est-ce que je peux laisser un message?

_____ **e.** — Bien sûr.

_____ **f.** — Non, elle n'est pas là. Vous pouvez rappeler plus tard?

_____ **g.** — D'accord. Au revoir.

SCORE ______

B. Choose the most logical ending from the box below for each of the following sentences. (4 points)

a. répondre aux questions du prof.
e. étudies à la bibliothèque.
d. n'aime pas les sports d'hiver.
c. perds toujours tes devoirs.
b. Pamela au cinéma.
f. n'aimes pas le sport.

_____ **1.** Claire va vendre ses skis. Elle...

_____ **2.** Nous attendons...

_____ **3.** Tu vas rater ton interro d'anglais parce que tu...

_____ **4.** Je suis très timide. Je n'aime pas...

SCORE ______

Nom ______________________ Classe ______________ Date ______________

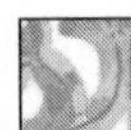

Alternative Quiz 9-2A

C. Tell what these people did yesterday using the verb in parentheses. (8 points)

1. Je/J' ______________ (perdre) mon cahier de maths.
2. Véronique ______________ (répondre) à la lettre de sa grand-mère.
3. Vous ______________ (vendre) vos vélos.
4. Nous ______________ (attendre) vingt minutes devant le cinéma.

SCORE

D. Complete each of the sentences below with the correct present tense form of the verb in parentheses. (16 points)

1. Vous ______________ le bus. (attendre)
2. Je ______________ toujours mes devoirs. (perdre)
3. Tu ______________ des fleurs sur le marché. (vendre)
4. Nous ______________ au téléphone quand mes parents ne sont pas là. (répondre)
5. Jérôme et Nicolas, vous ______________ toujours vos portefeuilles! (perdre)
6. Je téléphone à Li, mais ça ne ______________ pas. (répondre)
7. Gabrielle ______________ son vélo. (vendre)
8. Odile et Pascal ______________ aux questions du prof. (répondre)

SCORE

TOTAL SCORE /35

CHAPITRE 9

CHAPITRE 9

Nom________________ Classe__________ Date__________

Au téléphone

Alternative Quiz 9-3A

TROISIEME ETAPE

Maximum Score: 35/100

Grammar and Vocabulary

A. Several of your friends are asking for advice about problems they have. Choose the most logical response to each of their problems. (10 points)

_____ 1. Je veux aller à une boum ce soir, mais je n'ai pas de robe.

_____ 2. J'ai oublié mon déjeuner à la maison.

_____ 3. Je ne comprends pas l'algèbre!

_____ 4. Mon frère veut aller à Paris cet été, mais il n'a pas d'argent.

_____ 5. Je n'ai pas vu ma copine depuis deux semaines.

a. Achète-les!
b. Pourquoi il ne travaille pas?
c. Parle-leur!
d. Mange à la cantine!
e. Téléphone-lui!
f. Tu devrais parler au prof.
g. Oublie-le!
h. Tu devrais aller au centre commercial.

SCORE _____

B. You're working for the school newspaper. The letters that several students wrote to the advice columnist **Chère Mathilde** have got mixed up with the responses, and you're trying to sort them out. Place the phrases below in the appropriate column. (5 points)

Pourquoi tu ne leur téléphones pas?
Ne t'en fais pas!
Qu'est-ce que je peux faire?
Tu devrais parler à tes parents.
J'ai un petit problème.

STUDENT	CHERE MATHILDE
__________	__________
__________	__________
__________	__________
__________	__________

SCORE _____

CHAPITRE 9

Nom ______________________ Classe ______________ Date ______________

Alternative Quiz 9-3A

C. Complete these conversations by circling the correct pronouns. (10 points)

1. — Ma copine travaille à Madrid pendant tout l'été.
   — Tu devrais (lui/leur) téléphoner.
2. — J'ai acheté de jolies fleurs au marché.
   — Montre-(les/leur) moi!
3. — Pauline est super sympa.
   — Alors, invite-(la/le) à ta boum.
4. — Je n'ai pas encore fait la vaisselle.
   — Tu devrais (les/la) faire tout de suite.
5. — Je ne comprends pas du tout mes parents.
   — Pourquoi tu ne (lui/leur) parles pas?

SCORE ______

D. Read these statements and circle the person or thing that each pronoun is replacing. (10 points)

1. Je les cherche depuis longtemps.
   a. ma calculatrice **b.** mes livres **c.** ma montre
2. Tu devrais lui répondre.
   a. Clara et Patrick **b.** la lettre **c.** ta grand-mère
3. Il va le prendre.
   a. le coca **b.** la limonade **c.** les cafés
4. Pourquoi tu ne les achètes pas?
   a. ces baskets **b.** cette jupe **c.** ce tee-shirt
5. Elle est mignonne. Invite-la!
   a. Xavier **b.** Delphine **c.** Emilie et Sarah

SCORE ______

TOTAL SCORE ______ /35

Nom ______________________ Classe ______________ Date ______________

CHAPITRE 10

Dans un magasin de vêtements

PREMIERE ETAPE

Alternative Quiz 10-1A

Maximum Score: 35/100

Grammar and Vocabulary

A. You're trying to arrange your closet according to the seasons. Put each item in the proper section. (11 points)

une mini-jupe **un short** **un pull** **un cardigan** **des sandales** **un blouson** **une écharpe** **un manteau** **un maillot de bain** **un sweat-shirt** **des bottes**

Pour l'hiver	Pour l'été
______________________	______________________
______________________	______________________
______________________	______________________
______________________	______________________
______________________	______________________
______________________	______________________
______________________	______________________

SCORE

B. You're in charge of selecting the costumes for the school play. Pick the outfits that would be the most logical for each of the following characters. (6 points)

_____ **1.** Monsieur Proust qui travaille au bureau

_____ **2.** Julie qui est toujours à la piscine

_____ **3.** Madame Lemaire qui va à l'opéra

_____ **4.** Guillaume qui adore faire du ski

_____ **5.** Marion qui va au lycée

_____ **6.** Nicolas qui joue au football

a. des baskets et un short

b. un maillot de bain et des lunettes de soleil

c. une écharpe et un blouson

d. une robe et des boucles d'oreilles

e. un jean et un pull

f. une cravate et une veste

SCORE

Alternative Quiz 10-1A

C. You're writing an article about the gala organized by the French club last weekend, and you're taking notes on what everyone wore. Make complete sentences in the **passé composé** using the cues provided. (4 points)

1. Leah ______________________ (porter) une robe.
2. Coralie et Donna ______________________ (mettre) une jupe.
3. Patrick et moi, nous ______________________ (mettre) une veste.
4. Vous ______________________ (porter) une chemise.

SCORE ______

D. Use the cues provided and write complete sentences to tell what these people are or are not wearing. Be sure to make all the necessary changes. (14 points)

1. Elle / mettre / montre

____

2. Tu / ne...pas mettre / chaussettes

____

3. Je / mettre / pull / rouge

____

4. Nous / porter / bottes

____

5. Elles / mettre / beaucoup / bracelets

____

6. Thierry / mettre / cravate

____

7. Vous / ne...pas porter / ceintures

____

SCORE ______

TOTAL SCORE ______ /35

Nom _______________ Classe _______________ Date _______________

Dans un magasin de vêtements

Alternative Quiz 10-2A 

DEUXIEME ETAPE

Maximum Score: 30/100

Grammar and Vocabulary

A. Tell the saleswoman that you prefer the items she's showing you in another color. Do not repeat the item in your answers. (4 points)

1. — Nous avons des chaussures marron.

   — Je préfère _______________ *(the blue ones).*

2. — Voici des chemisiers roses.

   — Je préfère _______________ *(the purple ones).*

3. — Vous aimez la jupe rouge?

   — Je préfère _______________ *(the green one).*

4. — Voici un pantalon noir.

   — Je préfère _______________ *(the white one).*

SCORE ☐

B. Fill in the blank with the appropriate present tense form of the verb in parentheses. (6 points)

1. Vous _______________ (maigrir) quand vous ne mangez pas de chocolat.
2. Jean-Paul _______________ (choisir) un livre de science-fiction.
3. Les enfants _______________ (grandir) chaque année.
4. Je _______________ (grossir) quand je ne joue pas au foot.
5. Nous _______________ (maigrir) en été.
6. Tu _______________ (choisir) un steak-frites.

SCORE ☐

Nom ______________________ Classe ____________ Date ____________

Alternative Quiz 10-2A

CHAPITRE 10

C. Use the suggested phrases to complete these conversations that you might hear at a clothing boutique. (20 points)

1. — ______________ quelque chose ______________
   (I'd like) *(to go with)*

   cette jupe. ______________ ce chemisier?
   (Can I try on?)

2. — ______________ quelque chose ______________ pour l'été.
   (I need) *(in cotton)*

   — Nous avons ces pantalons et ces chemisiers.

3. — Vous désirez?

   — ______________________________
   (I'm just looking.)

4. — Est-ce que je peux vous aider?

   — Oui, ______________________ aller à l'opéra.
   (I'm looking for something to)

   — Regardez ces jupes en cuir.

   — Vous les avez ______________________?
   (in cotton)

5. — Excusez-moi, madame ______________________
   (do you have that in 34?)

   — Je ne sais pas. Je vais voir.

6. — J'adore le manteau dans la vitrine! ______________________
   (How much is it?)

   — C'est 145€.

SCORE

TOTAL SCORE /30

CHAPITRE 10

Nom ______________ Classe ______________ Date ______________

Dans un magasin de vêtements

Alternative Quiz 10-3A 

TROISIEME ETAPE

Maximum Score: 35/100

Grammar and Vocabulary

A. Read the statements below, and then, in the sentences that follow, replace the underlined words with the appropriate direct object pronoun. (5 points)

1. Elle déteste cette cravate. Elle ____________ déteste.
2. Il choisit les chaussettes rouges. Il ____________ choisit.
3. Tu as trouvé le blouson. Tu ____________ as trouvé.
4. Je vais prendre cette ceinture. Je vais ____________ prendre.
5. Vous détestez ce film. Vous ____________ détestez.

SCORE

B. Marthe and her brother, Roger, are trying to buy a birthday gift for their mother, but they always have opposite opinions. Complete their conversation with the appropriate adjectives from the box. Use a different adjective each time. (10 points)

petit courte serrée jolie démodée
beau horrible chouette

MARTHE Comment tu trouves cette robe Roger? Elle est très à la mode, non?

ROGER Mais non! Elle est **(1)** ____________________.

MARTHE Ben, ce blouson est joli mais un peu grand.

ROGER Au contraire! Je le trouve **(2)** ____________________. Tu aimes cette veste? Elle est un peu large, mais je l'aime bien.

MARTHE Non, elle est trop **(3)** ____________________.

MARTHE Regarde cette écharpe, elle est sensass!

ROGER Pas du tout! Elle est vraiment **(4)** ____________________!

ROGER Alors, prenons cette jupe bleue. Elle est assez longue. Maman va l'adorer.

MARTHE Ecoute Roger, la jupe est trop **(5)** ____________________. Maman ne va pas porter de mini-jupe quand même!

SCORE

Nom ______________________ Classe ______________ Date ______________

CHAPITRE 10

Alternative Quiz 10-3A

C. You're at the school cafeteria in France. Complete these snippets of conversations you overhear with **Il/Elle est, Ils/Elles sont** or **C'est.** (10 points)

1. — Pourquoi tu n'achètes pas cet ordinateur?

   — ______________________ trop cher!

2. — Oh, je n'aime plus ce blouson. Il n'est pas beau.

   — Oui, ______________________ un peu large.

3. — Comment tu trouves ma jupe en cuir?

   — ______________________ cool!

4. — J'adore tes boucles d'oreilles. ______________________ mignonnes.

   — Tu trouves?

5. — Tu aimes porter un jean à l'école?

   — Oui, ______________________ très confortable.

SCORE ______

D. You're at the mall with some friends. Answer their questions according to the cues below. Use the appropriate direct object pronoun in your responses. (10 points)

1. Tu mets tes bottes en hiver?

   Oui, ____

2. Tu prends la chemise blanche?

   Oui, ____

3. Tu prends le blouson vert?

   Non, ____

4. Tu préfères ces baskets bleues?

   Oui, ____

5. Tu aimes ce short?

   Oui, ____

SCORE ______

TOTAL SCORE ______ /35

CHAPITRE 11

Nom _______________ Classe _______________ Date _______________

Vive les vacances!

Alternative Quiz 11-1A

PREMIERE ETAPE

Maximum Score: 40/100

Grammar and Vocabulary

A. Georges and Stéphane are talking about their plans for the upcoming vacation. Complete their conversation using the cues provided. (12 points)

— (1) _______________ pendant les vancances d'été?
(Where are you going to go)

— En juillet, (2) _______________ aller à la campagne pour
(I feel like)

(3) _______________ . Et toi? (4) _______________?
(to go hiking) *(What are you going to do)*

— Je vais (5) _______________ et (6) _______________.
(to windsurf) *(to go sailing)*.

SCORE

B. You're looking at an agenda for a world tour in a traveling brochure, but some of the print is not very legible. Write **à**, **au**, **aux**, or **en** in front of each place. (14 points)

Nous allons aller (1) _____ Tokyo, (2) _____ Etats-Unis, (3) _____ Miami, (4) _____ Canada, (5) _____ Brésil, (6) _____ Sénégal, (7) _____ Maroc, (8) _____ Espagne, (9) _____ France, (10) _____ Berlin, (11) _____ Italie, (12) _____ Egypte, (13) _____ Viêt-nam et (14) _____ Chine.

SCORE

C. You're checking the plans for next weekend. Write complete sentences in French, using the cues provided, to tell what you and your friends are going to do. Don't forget to use the appropriate form of the verb **aller**. (8 points)

1. Loïc et Stéphane (going to their grandmother's house)

____

2. Tu (going to the forest)

____

3. Michelle (going to the countryside)

____

CHAPITRE 11

Alternative Quiz 11-1A

4. Martin et moi (sailing)

____

SCORE

D. Jérôme is telling you about the things he likes to do. Using the activities in the box and the illustrations, suggest where he can go to do these activities. Use each activity only once. (6 points)

faire de la plongée **faire du ski** **faire de l'équitation et jouer au volley**

1. 

Tu peux ____

____.

2. 

Tu peux ____

____.

3. 

Tu peux ____

____.

SCORE

TOTAL SCORE /40

CHAPITRE 11

Nom ______________________ Classe ______________ Date ______________

Vive les vacances!

Alternative Quiz 11-2A

DEUXIEME ETAPE

Maximum Score: 30/100

Grammar and Vocabulary

A. Your friends are telling you about their problems. Suggest some solutions using the command forms of the verb in parentheses. (5 points)

1. Anne didn't get good grades in French.

   (sortir) ______________________ moins avec tes amis!

2. Eddie and Patricia always arrive late to school.

   (prendre) ______________________ le bus de 7h!

3. Alice has been working for six months straight.

   (partir) ______________________ en vacances!

4. Brian and Michael are bored.

   (faire) ______________________ une boum avec vos amis!

5. Jacob is always tired.

   (dormir) ______________________ plus la nuit!

SCORE

B. You and a friend are telling each other riddles. Write, in French, the name of the object that your friend is describing. (7 points)

1. You buy this for your friends and family on special occasions. ______________
2. You need this to travel to many foreign countries. ______________
3. You use this to make lasting images. ______________
4. You need this to travel by train. ______________
5. You need this to carry your clothes when you travel. ______________
6. You use this when it's raining. ______________
7. You need this to travel by plane from New York to L.A. ______________

SCORE

CHAPITRE 11

Nom ______________________ Classe ______________ Date ______________

Alternative Quiz 11-2A

C. You overhear several conversations of people saying goodbye at the airport. Complete their conversations using the cues provided. (10 points)

1. — ______________________ de m'envoyer une carte postale.
(Don't forget)

— D'accord.

2. — ______________________ de faire une réservation à l'hôtel?
(You didn't forget)

— Non, ______________________.
(Don't worry)

3. — ______________________! Au revoir.
(Have a good vacation)

— Au revoir. ______________________!
(Have fun)

SCORE [ ]

CHAPITRE 11

D. After a great Thanksgiving dinner you're recording in your journal everyone's plans for the rest of the evening. Fill in each blank with the appropriate present tense form of the verb in parentheses. (8 points)

Ma grand-mère **(1)** ______________ (dormir) chez nous ce soir. Elle prend ma chambre. Alors, ce soir, je **(2)** ______________ (dormir) sur le sofa. Ma grand-mère ne prend jamais la chambre de mon frère, Roger, alors il **(3)** ______________ (dormir) toujours dans sa chambre.

Mon oncle Gérard et ma tante Marthe **(4)** ______________ (partir) ce soir, mais Lucie, ma cousine, **(5)** ______________ (partir) demain. Elle **(6)** ______________ (sortir) avec nous ce soir. Ma cousine et moi, nous allons au cinéma. Nous **(7)** ______________ (sortir) souvent ensemble. Roger et ses amis ne **(8)** ______________ (sortir) jamais avec nous. Ils aiment aller au théâtre, aux musées et aux cafés. Moi, je trouve ça barbant! Bon, je dois partir maintenant.

SCORE [ ]

TOTAL SCORE [/30]

Nom ______________ Classe ______________ Date ______________

Vive les vacances!

Alternative Quiz 11-3A

Maximum Score: 30/100

TROISIEME ETAPE

Grammar and Vocabulary

A. Fill in the blanks with the correct **passé composé** form of the verb in parentheses. (10 points)

1. Je/J' ______________ (oublier) mon argent!
2. Cet été, nous ______________ (faire) un voyage en Italie.
3. Hier, Claude ______________ (trouver) un cadeau pour Maman.
4. Céline et toi, vous ______________ (parler) au téléphone hier soir.
5. Ce matin, elles ______________ (prendre) un taxi pour aller au lycée.

SCORE

B. Rearrange the events in Michel's day in a logical order. Use letters **a-e.** Mark the first event with the letter **a** and so on. (5 points)

_____ 1. Finalement, nous avons dîné dans un restaurant chinois.

_____ 2. D'abord, j'ai lavé la voiture.

_____ 3. Après, Martine et moi, nous avons fait une promenade au parc.

_____ 4. Ensuite, j'ai téléphoné à Martine et nous sommes allés au centre commercial.

_____ 5. J'ai acheté des romans français et une chemise rouge en soie.

SCORE

Nom ______________________ Classe ______________ Date ______________

Alternative Quiz 11-3A

C. Circle the phrase that doesn't belong in each group. (5 points)

1. Oh, c'était ennuyeux.
   C'était épouvantable.
   Oh, pas mauvais.

2. Très chouette.
   C'était ennuyeux.
   C'était formidable!

3. Tu as passé un bon été?
   Tu t'es bien amusé?
   Tu t'appelles comment?

4. C'était épouvantable.
   C'était un véritable cauchemar.
   C'était très chouette.

5. Oui, très chouette!
   Oui, c'était formidable!
   C'était épouvantable.

SCORE [ ]

D. Write what your friends might say about their vacation, based on what they did. Choose from the expressions in the word box below. (10 points)

C'était formidable!	Oh, pas mauvais.	C'était un véritable cauchemar!

1. Sophie adore la ville *(city)*, mais elle a passé l'été à la campagne avec ses amies.
   ____

2. Tonio adore faire du camping et il est allé en forêt avec son père.
   ____

3. Jérôme déteste la plage et il est allé au bord de la mer avec ses parents.
   ____

4. Sarah aime faire de la planche à voile et elle est allée au bord de la mer.
   ____

5. Marie aime faire de la randonnée, mais elle préfère faire de la plongée. Elle est allée à la montagne.
   ____

SCORE [ ]

TOTAL SCORE [/30]

CHAPITRE 11

Nom ______________ Classe ______________ Date ______________

En ville

Alternative Quiz 12-1A 

PREMIERE ETAPE

Maximum Score: 35/100

Grammar and Vocabulary

A. Your pen pal, Mireille Lemaire, wrote to you about her weekend plans. Parts of her letter are not readable. Fill in the blanks with **au, à la, à l'**, or **aux.** (7 points)

Samedi soir, Marc vient dîner chez moi. Je vais préparer un gâteau. Alors, le matin, je dois aller (1) ______________ supermarché pour acheter des œufs et de la farine. Tu sais, Marc va passer cet été (2) ______________ Canada chez son oncle Jim. Il part dimanche matin, donc, samedi, il va passer la nuit (3) ______________ maison.

Dimanche, je vais aller (4) ______________ gare avec Marc, et après, je vais retrouver Armand (5) ______________ café. Nous avons décidé d'aller (6) ______________ plage. Nous allons faire une promenade. Dimanche soir, je vais aller (7) ______________ au cinéma avec Sophie.

SCORE ______

B. Your friend needs to do the following errands. Write the name of the place where he or she needs to go. (12 points)

1. acheter un kilo de tomates ______________
2. acheter des médicaments ______________
3. acheter un CD ______________
4. acheter des enveloppes ______________
5. acheter un gâteau au chocolat ______________
6. acheter une baguette ______________

SCORE ______

Nom ______________________ Classe ______________ Date ______________

Alternative Quiz 12-1A

C. Write two errands that you can do in each of these places. (12 points)

1. POSTE ______________________________

   ____

2. BANQUE ______________________________

   ____

3. BIBLIOTHEQUE ______________________________

   ____

SCORE [ ]

D. Your friend is showing you pictures of his new house. Complete your conversation below with the appropriate expressions. (4 points)

— Tu veux voir des photos de ma maison?

— Oui, bien sûr!

— Alors, (1) ______________________ *(Look, there is)* ma pièce *(room)* préférée, la salle à manger.

Et (2) ______________________ *(there, you see)* c'est la salle de séjour.

(3) ______________________ *(Here is)* ma chambre et (4) ______________________ *(there, that is)* la salle de bains.

SCORE [ ]

TOTAL SCORE [/35]

CHAPITRE 12

CHAPITRE 12

Nom_______________ Classe_______________ Date_______________

En ville

Alternative Quiz 12-2A

DEUXIEME ETAPE

Maximum Score: 30/100

Grammar and Vocabulary

A. Frédéric is asking his sister if she can run some errands for him in town. Rearrange their conversation in a logical order by numbering them from 1 to 5. (5 points)

_____ **a** — D'accord. Moi aussi, j'ai besoin de timbres.

_____ **b** — Frédéric, je vais en ville. Il te faut quelque chose?

_____ **c** — Oui, tu pourrais passer à la bibliothèque?

_____ **d** — Tu peux aussi aller à la poste?

_____ **e** — Si tu veux.

SCORE

B. Write, in French, how you would travel, if you used the following means of transportation. (10 points)

1.  _______________

2.  _______________

3.  _______________

4.  _______________

5.  _______________

SCORE

CHAPITRE 12

Nom ______________________ Classe ______________ Date ______________

Alternative Quiz 12-2A

C. Your mother made a list of things for you to do today. Fill in the blanks with the appropriate form: **de l', de la, du, des,** or **de.** (5 points)

D'abord, va à la banque pour retirer **(1)** ____________ argent. Après, va à la papeterie et achète **(2)** ____________ enveloppes. Passe à la poste, parce que nous n'avons plus **(3)** ____________ timbres. Puis, passe à l'épicerie de M. Duchamp et achète **(4)** ____________ jambon et **(5)** ____________ confiture.

SCORE

D. Rewrite these sentences using the pronoun **y.** (10 points)

1. Hier, nous avons rencontré Vincent au marché.
   ____
2. Jérôme et Martin n'aiment pas aller au stade.
   ____
3. Marie-France achète du beurre à l'épicerie.
   ____
4. Je suis allé à la banque pour déposer un chèque.
   ____
5. Tonio va aller à la bibliothèque pour emprunter un livre.
   ____
6. Je vais passer à la boulangerie pour acheter du pain.
   ____
7. On va très souvent au parc.
   ____
8. Elles ont acheté leurs livres à la librairie hier.
   ____
9. Vous allez acheter des timbres à la poste.
   ____
10. Tu ne vas pas à la pharmacie aujourd'hui?
    ____

SCORE TOTAL SCORE /30

Nom ____________________ Classe ______________ Date ______________

12 En ville

Alternative Quiz 12-3A 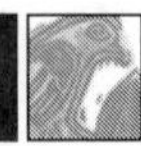

TROISIEME ETAPE

Maximum Score: 35/100

Grammar and Vocabulary

A. Vincent and Stuart are discussing the shortest way to get to the park. Complete their conversation. Be sure to use the **tu** form. (10 points)

— D'ici, **(1)** ____________________ *(you keep going)* jusqu'au prochain feu rouge. Là, **(2)** ________________ *(you turn)* à gauche et voilà le parc.

— Mais non! **(3)** ____________________ *(Take . . . street)* Victor Hugo, (4) ________________ *(then cross)* le boulevard Ste-Croix. **(5)** ____________________ *(You'll pass)* la boulangerie et le parc est juste en face.

SCORE ☐

B. Philippe is talking about the layout of his hometown. Fill in the blanks with the appropriate form: **des, du, de la,** or **de l'.** (5 points)

Au centre de la ville, il y a un grand parc. Au nord **(1)** __________ parc, il y a une banque. A côté **(2)** __________ banque, il y a un supermarché. A gauche **(3)** __________ supermarché, il y a un lycée. En face **(4)** __________ lycée, il y a beaucoup de maisons. Pas loin **(5)** __________ maisons, il y a le stade.

SCORE ☐

C. Complete the conversation between Antoine and a tourist using the cues provided. (10 points)

— (1) ______________________________ *(Excuse me)* monsieur.

(2) ______________________________ *(I'm looking for)* la poste,

(3) ______________________________ *(please)* ?

— Oui, alors, **(4)** ______________________________ *(you go straight ahead until you get to)* lycée.

(5) ______________________________ *(It's right there on the)* droite.

SCORE ☐

Nom ______________________ Classe ____________ Date ____________

Alternative Quiz 12-3A

D. Based on the map of your pen pal's hometown, fill in the blanks with the appropriate preposition from the box below. Use a different preposition each time. (10 points)

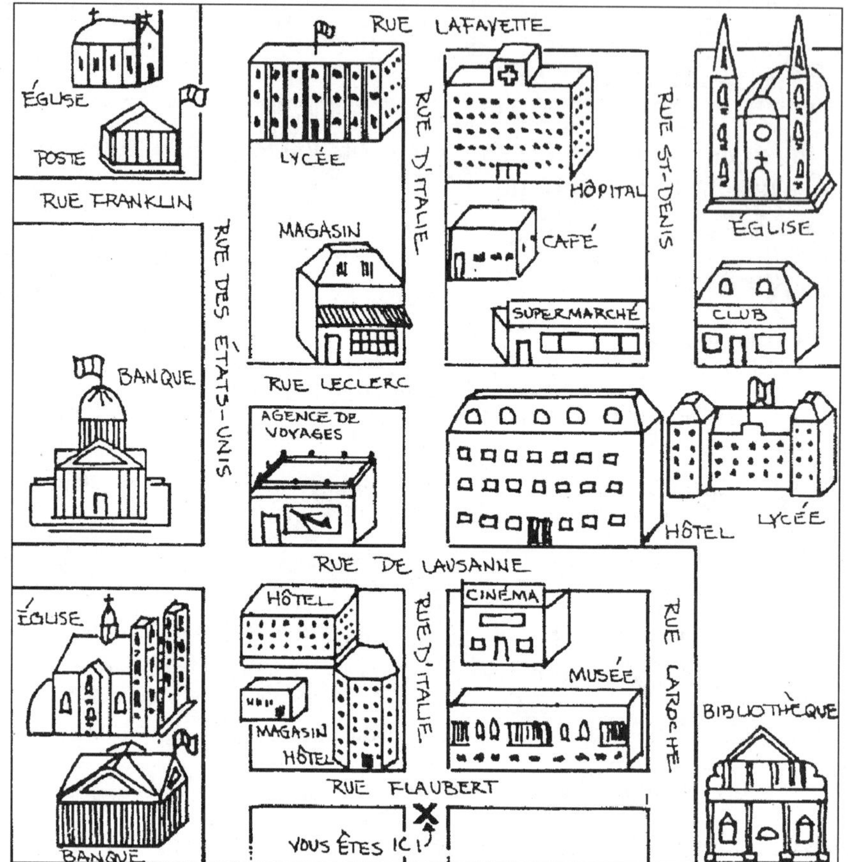

loin	devant	entre	au coin	derrière
à côté de	à gauche de	à droite de	près	

1. Le café est ____________________ le supermarché et l'hôpital.
2. Le club est ____________________ l'église.
3. La poste est ____________________ de la bibliothèque.
4. Le cinéma est ____________________ le musée.
5. L'agence de voyages est ____________________ du supermarché.

SCORE [ ]

TOTAL SCORE [/35]

CHAPITRE 12

Answer Key

Answers to Alternative Quizzes 1-1A, 1-2A, and 1-3A

Alternative Quiz 1-1A

A. (5 points: 1 point per item)
1. très bien
2. pas terrible
3. bof
4. très bien
5. comme ci comme ça

B. (5 points: 1 point per item)
1. Salut
2. Pas mal
3. Et toi
4. il s'appelle
5. A tout à l'heure

C. (5 points: 1 point per item)
1. Bonjour!
2. Salut!
3. Salut!
4. Salut!
5. Bonjour!

D. (10 points: 2 points per item)
Possible answers:
1. Bonjour! Ça va? / Bonjour! Je m'appelle _____.
2. Ça va. / Ça va bien.
3. Je m'appelle _____.
4. J'ai _____ ans.
5. Tchao! / Salut!

E. (10 points: 1 point per item)

1. vingt	6. huit
2. deux	7. dix-sept
3. quinze	8. douze
4. quatorze	9. dix-neuf
5. dix	10. treize

Alternative Quiz 1-2A

A. (6 points: 1 point per item)
1. le; 2. le; 3. la; 4. l'; 5. le; 6. les

B. (6 points: 1 point per item)
1. les frites; n'aime pas
2. J'aime bien; je préfère
3. l'école
4. le français

C. (8 points: 2 points per item)
1. Non, je n'aime pas la glace.
2. Non, je n'aime pas la plage.
3. Non, je n'aime pas le sport.
4. Non, je n'aime pas les vacances.

D. (10 points: 1 point per item)
1. soccer; the beach
2. math
3. soccer
4. movies
5. the beach
6. sports
7. English; chocolate
8. vacation

Alternative Quiz 1-3A

A. (7 points: 1 point per item)
1. les vacances
2. écouter de la musique
3. faire les magasins
4. lire
5. faire de l'équitation
6. faire du sport
7. danser

B. (8 points: 2 points per item)
1. Oui, ils aiment faire les magasins.
2. Oui, elles aiment faire du sport.
3. Oui, il adore regarder la télé.
4. Oui, elle aime lire.

C. (10 points: 2 points per item)
1. étudiez
2. écoutons
3. dansent
4. adore
5. voyagent

D. (10 points: 2 points per item)
1. Bertrand likes to listen to music, but he prefers to go out with his friends. He also likes to ride horses, but he loves swimming. He also likes vacations because he likes to travel.
2. He likes to listen to music and going out with his friends.
3. He likes horseback riding and swimming.
4. He doesn't mention an activity he doesn't like.
5. He likes vacations because he likes to travel.

Answers to Alternative Quizzes 2-1A, 2-2A, and 2-3A

Alternative Quiz 2-1A

A. (5 points: 1 point per item)

1.	la chorale	**2.**	la physique
3.	l'histoire	**4.**	la géographie
5.	l'allemand		

B. (10 points: 1 point per item)

1.	le français	**6.**	la chimie
2.	l'informatique	**7.**	l'espagnol
3.	la géométrie	**8.**	la danse
4.	l'histoire	**9.**	le latin
5.	l'algèbre	**10.**	le sport

C. (5 points: 1 point per item)
1. Moi, si.
2. Moi aussi.
3. Moi non plus.
4. Pas moi.
5. Non, pas trop.

D. (10 points: 2 points per item)
1. Oui, j'aime l'espagnol.
2. Si, nous aimons les sciences naturelles.
3. Si, elles aiment les examens.
4. Si, il aime le latin.
5. Oui, ils aiment le prof.

Alternative Quiz 2-2A

A. (4 points: 1 point per item)
1. onze heures
2. cinq heures quinze
3. seize heures vingt-cinq
4. dix-huit heures quarante-cinq

B. (7 points: 1 point per item)

1.	samedi	**5.**	dimanche
2.	mardi	**6.**	mercredi
3.	vendredi	**7.**	jeudi
4.	lundi		

C. (4 points: 1 point per item)
1. quels cours
2. J'ai
3. vous avez
4. nous avons

D. (8 points: 1 point per item)
1. f; **2.** d; **3.** a; **4.** h; **5.** i; **6.** b; **7.** c; **8.** g

E. (6 points: 1 point per item)
1. trente-deux
2. cinquante-neuf
3. vingt-sept
4. cinquante-trois
5. quarante-cinq
6. quarante et un

F. (6 points: 1 point per item)
1. a; **2.** as; **3.** avez; **4.** ont; **5.** avons; **6.** ai

Alternative Quiz 2-3A

A. (10 points: 2 points per item)
1. cool
2. zéro
3. difficile
4. difficile
5. facile

B. (15 points: 1 point per item)
To express an unfavorable opinion:
zéro; pas génial; nul; pas super; pas terrible; barbant
To express indifference:
bof; comme ci comme ça; pas mal
To express a favorable opinion:
facile; super; intéressant; passionnant; génial; cool

C. (6 points: 1 point per item)
1. L; **2.** D; **3.** L; **4.** L; **5.** D; **6.** L

D. (4 points: 1 point per item)
1. a; **2.** b; **3.** a; **4.** b.

Answers to Alternative Quizzes 3-1A, 3-2A, and 3-3A

Alternative Quiz 3-1A

A. (10 points: 1 point per item)
1. une; **2.** des; **3.** un; **4.** des; **5.** une
6. de; **7.** une; **8.** des; **9.** de; **10.** une

B. (10 points: 1 point per item)
You: une gomme, un taille-crayon, un sac à dos
Jacob: une trousse, un classeur
Alain: un cahier, une calculatrice, une règle
Renato: des feuilles de papier, un livre

C. (5 points: 1 point per item)
1. des livres
2. des classeurs
3. des calculatrices
4. des trousses
5. des règles / des stylos

D. (10 points: 2 points per item)
1. Non, je n'ai pas de calculatrice.
2. Non, je n'ai pas de feuilles de papier.
3. Non, nous n'avons pas de cahiers.
4. Non, je n'ai pas de stylo.
5. Non, nous n'avons pas de crayons.

Alternative Quiz 3-2A

A. (6 points: 1 point per item)
1. des baskets
2. un ordinateur
3. une télévision
4. un magazine
5. un poster
6. une radio

B. (7 points: 1 point per item)
1. cette; **2.** cette; **3.** ce; **4.** ces;
5. ce; **6.** ce; **7.** ce

C. (14 points: 2 points per item)
1. blancs; **2.** violette; **3.** noirs; **4.** bleue
5. grises; **6.** rouges; **7.** verts

D. (3 points: 1/2 point per item)
1. a; **2.** g; **3.** i; **4.** b; **5.** f; **6.** e

Alternative Quiz 3-3A

A. (20 points: 2 points per item)
1. six cent un
2. deux cent soixante-dix-neuf
3. neuf cent quatre-vingt-dix-neuf
4. trois cent soixante-treize
5. trois cent quatre-vingt-cinq
6. cinq cents
7. six cent dix-sept
8. deux cent soixante-sept
9. sept cent quatre-vingt-quatorze
10. quatre-vingt-treize

B. (5 points: 1 point per item)
1. Excusez-moi
2. C'est combien
3. C'est
4. Merci
5. A votre service

C. (10 points: 1 point per item)
1. 75
2. 180
3. 478
4. 74
5. 942
6. 952
7. 890
8. 246
9. 88
10. 529

Answers to Alternative Quizzes 4-1A, 4-2A, and 4-3A

ANSWERS Alternative Quiz 4-1A

A. (10 points: 1 point per item)
INDIVIDUAL SPORTS
faire du jogging; faire du roller en ligne; jouer au golf; faire du vélo; faire de l'athlétisme
TEAM SPORTS
jouer au football; jouer au volley; jouer au hockey
WATER ACTIVITIES
faire de la natation; faire du ski nautique

B. (5 points: 1 point per item)
1. d; **2.** a; **3.** f; **4.** b; **5.** c

C. (10 points: 1 point per item)
1. faire; **2.** du; **3.** faire; **4.** jouer; **5.** au
6. de la; **7.** faire; **8.** faire; **9.** au; **10.** du

D. (10 points: 2 points per item)
1. Est-ce que Paul et toi, vous adorez faire du ski?
2. Est-ce que Charles et Gilles adorent nager?
3. Est-ce que Pierre aime jouer aux cartes ou est-ce qu'il préfère jouer au hockey?
4. Est-ce que tu aimes faire du vélo?
5. Est-ce qu'Onélia aime bien lire?

Alternative Quiz 4-2A

A. (8 points: 1 point per item)
1. fait; **2.** faites; **3.** faisons; **4.** fais
5. font; **6.** fais; **7.** fais; **8.** faire

B. (4 points: 1 point per item)
1. Non, on ne joue pas au football américain en mai.
2. Non, on ne joue pas au base-ball en décembre.
3. Non, on ne fait pas de ski nautique au Canada en hiver.
4. Non, on ne fait pas de ski en Floride au printemps.

C. (10 points: 2 points per item)
1. il fait chaud; **2.** il pleut; **3.** il fait froid; **4.** il neige; **5.** il fait beau

D. (5 points: 1 point per item)
1. d; **2.** f; **3.** e; **4.** b; **5.** a

E. (8 points: 2 points per item)
1. Ils aiment jouer au base-ball.
2. Est-ce qu'elle parle français?
3. Je ne joue pas au volley.
4. Nous aimons faire du roller en ligne.

Alternative Quiz 4-3A

A. (6 points: 1 point per item)
1. faux; **2.** faux; **3.** faux; **4.** faux
5. vrai; **6.** faux

B. (12 points: 2 points per item)
1. Je fais de la natation de temps en temps.
2. Nous faisons de l'athlétisme une fois par semaine.
3. Vous ne faites jamais de vidéo.
4. Est-ce que tu fais souvent du ski?
5. Corinne et Nicole font quelquefois de la photo.
6. Ils font rarement du vélo.

C. (12 points: 3 points per item)
1. Julien fait souvent du vélo.
2. Julien fait quelquefois de la natation.
3. Odile fait du ski de temps en temps.
4. Patricia fait rarement du patin à glace.

Answers to Alternative Quizzes 5-1A, 5-2A, and 5-3A

Alternative Quiz 5-1A

A. (8 points: 2 points per item)
Possible answers:
1. Désolé(e), j'ai des trucs à faire.
2. D'accord! On va au cinéma.
3. Désolé(e), j'ai des courses à faire.
4. Bonne idée!

B. (8 points: 1 point per item)
Sandwiches:
1. un sandwich au jambon
2. un sandwich au saucisson
3. un croque-monsieur
4. un sandwich au fromage

Drinks:
1. une limonade
2. un sirop de fraise (à l'eau)
3. un jus d'orange
4. un coca

C. (6 points: 1 point per item)
1. prendre; **2.** prennent; **3.** prend
4. prenons; **5.** prends; **6.** prends

D. (8 points: 2 points per item)
1. On joue à des jeux vidéo?
2. On mange au restaurant?
3. On va au café?
4. On va à la piscine?

Alternative Quiz 5-2A

A. (16 points: 2 points per item)
1. Prends des photos!
2. Donnez les sandwiches aux élèves!
3. Parle au professeur!
4. Fais les sandwiches!
5. Apportez les boissons!
6. Faites attention!
7. Prenez des notes!
8. Regarde le tableau!

B. (10 points: 2 points per item)
1. Ecoute la radio!
2. Fais tes devoirs!
3. Mange un sandwich!
4. Joue au golf!
5. Prends une limonade!

C. (9 points: 1 point per item)
TO GET SOMEONE'S ATTENTION
Excusez-moi. Monsieur! Madame! Mademoiselle! La carte, s'il vous plaît!
TO ORDER FOOD AND BEVERAGES
Je voudrais un coca. Je vais prendre un hot-dog. Donnez-moi une limonade. Apportez-moi une crêpe.

Alternative Quiz 5-3A

A. (20 points: 2 points per item)
1. sept euros
2. neuf euros
3. onze euros
4. seize euros
5. quatre euros cinquante
6. douze euros
7. huit euros
8. treize euros
9. vingt euros
10. dix euros

B. (8 points: 2 points per item)
1. c'est combien
2. Ça fait combien
3. Oui, tout de suite
4. l'addition, s'il vous plaît

C. (7 points: 1 point per item)
TO TALK ABOUT A MEAL
C'est super.
C'est dégoûtant.
C'est pas bon.
C'est délicieux.
TO PAY FOR THE BILL
L'addition, s'il vous plaît.
Ça fait combien, s'il vous plaît?
C'est combien pour le hot-dog et le coca?

Answers to Alternative Quizzes 6-1A, 6-2A, and 6-3A

Alternative Quiz 6-1A

A. (10 points: 2 points per item)
Possible answers:
1. Va au centre commercial!
2. Va au cinéma!
3. Va à la plage!
4. Allez au parc!
5. Allez au parc! / Allez au stade!

B. (5 points: 1 point per item)
1. f; **2.** c; **3.** d; **4.** e; **5.** a

C. (10 points: 2 points per item)
1. Tu vas étudier pour le bac.
2. Nous allons faire un pique-nique au parc.
3. Nous allons parler au téléphone avec les copains.
4. Karine va faire du patin à glace dimanche.
5. Roger va faire les magasins samedi.

D. (5 points: 1 point per item)
1. allons; **2.** vont; **3.** va; **4.** vais; **5.** vas

ANSWERS

Alternative Quiz 6-2A

A. (12 points: 2 points per item)
1. Nous voulons voir un film dimanche soir.
2. Sophie et Laurent veulent aller à la piscine.
3. Je veux rester chez moi.
4. Tu veux regarder un match de foot-ball.
5. Nathalie et moi, nous voulons aller au zoo.
6. Gigi veut aller au centre commercial.

B. (5 points: 1 point per item)
1. Je; **2.** Nous; **3.** Ils; **4.** Elle; **5.** Vous

C. (8 points: 1point per item)
ACCEPT
Pourquoi pas?
Bonne idée.
Je veux bien.
D'accord.

REFUSE
J'ai des trucs à faire.
Ça ne me dit rien.
Désolé, je ne peux pas.
Désolée, je suis occupée.

D. (5 points: 1 point per item)
1. d; **2.** b; **3.** e; **4.** a; **5.** c

Alternative Quiz 6-3A

A. (12 points: 2 points per item)
1. deux heures vingt de l'après-midi
2. onze heures dix du matin
3. sept heures moins vingt du soir
4. huit heures moins cinq du matin
5. neuf heures moins dix du matin
6. six heures et quart du matin

B. (10 points: 1 point per item)
1. e; **2.** d / a; **3.** a; **4.** b; **5.** d / a
6. b; **7.** c; **8.** c; **9.** e; **10.** a

C. (8 points: 2 points per item)
Possible answers:
1. Avec qui est-ce que tu vas à la plage?
2. Quand est-ce que vous allez à la plage?
3. Où est-ce que vous allez vous retrouver?
4. A quelle heure est-ce que vous allez partir?

D. (10 points: 2 points per item)
1. Qu'est-ce que vous allez faire à 3:30 cet après-midi?
2. Où est-ce que vous allez mardi à midi?
3. Quand est-ce que vous allez au zoo?
4. A quelle heure est-ce qu'on se retrouve?
5. Avec qui est-ce que vous allez à la piscine?

Answers to Alternative Quizzes 7-1A, 7-2A, and 7-3A

ANSWERS Alternative Quiz 7-1A

A. (5 points: 1 point per item)
1. des; **2.** du; **3.** de la; **4.** de l'; **5.** du

B. (10 points: 1 point per item)
1. mes; **2.** leur; **3.** sa; **4.** nos; **5.** tes
6. sa; **7.** nos; **8.** tes; **9.** votre; **10.** mon

C. (20 points: 2 points per item)
1. Elle parle de son oncle.
2. Elle parle de son grand-père.
3. Elle parle de sa tante.
4. Elle parle de son père.
5. Elle parle de sa cousine.
6. Elle parle de sa mère.
7. Elle parle de son frère.
8. Elle parle de sa grand-mère.
9. Elle parle de sa tante.
10. Elle parle de sa tante.

Alternative Quiz 7-2A

A. (8 points: 1 point per item)

1. sympa	**5.** intéressants
2. fortes	**6.** gentille
3. blanches	**7.** âgées
4. grande	**8.** timides

B. (8 points: 1 point per item)
1. brun
2. gros
3. ni grand ni petit
4. sympa
5. petit
6. mince
7. intelligente
8. rousse

C. (8 points: 1 point per item)
1. êtes; **2.** es; **3.** sont; **4.** est
5. sommes; **6.** suis; **7.** sont; **8.** est

D. (6 points: 1 point per item)
1. méchants
2. passionnants
3. amusants
4. rousses
5. orange
6. petites

Alternative Quiz 7-3A

A. (8 points: 1 point per item)
ISABELLE
passer l'aspirateur
ranger les chambres
garder sa sœur
faire la vaisselle
ANGELE
faire les courses
promener le chien
tondre le gazon
laver la voiture

B. (12 points: 2 points per item)
1. Est-ce que Paul aime faire la vaisselle?
2. Martine n'est pas gentille.
3. Tu ranges ta chambre le samedi.
4. Mon cousin n'aime pas débarrasser la table.
5. Mon père et mon frère tondent le gazon chaque week-end.
6. Ma sœur et moi, nous promenons le chien quelquefois.

C. (8 points: 1 point per item)
ASKING FOR PERMISSION
Tu es d'accord?
Je peux sortir?
GIVING PERMISSION
D'accord.
Bien sûr!
Si tu veux.
REFUSING PERMISSION
C'est impossible.
Pas ce soir.
Pas question!

D. (7 points: 1 point per item)
1. Martine
2. do housework
3. Fabien and Jérôme
4. Antoinette
5. clean the bedrooms
6. Olivier
7. Julien

Answers to Alternative Quizzes 8-1A, 8-2A, and 8-3A

Alternative Quiz 8-1A

A. (10 points: 1 point per item)
  1. du; du; une
  2. de la; du; du
  3. une; des; des; un

B. (15 points: 1 point per item)
Gabrielle
du lait; des yaourts; du fromage; du porc; du bœuf
Agnès
des fraises; des papayes; des mangues; des pêches; des goyaves; des ananas
Cédric
du maïs; des pommes de terre; des haricots verts; des champignons

C. (5 points: 1 point per item)
  1. le maïs; **2.** le riz; **3.** les oignons
  4. le bœuf; **5.** les goyaves

D. (5 points: 1 point per item)
  1. a; **2.** c; **3.** b; **4.** b; 5. c

Alternative Quiz 8-2A

A. (6 points: 1 point per item)
  1. peux; **2.** pouvez; peux
  3. peut; **4.** peuvent; **5.** pouvons

B. (12 points: 2 points per item)
  1. Achète-moi deux kilos de porc!
  2. Voici huit tranches de jambon.
  3. Donne-moi trois boîtes de pêches!
  4. Je voudrais une douzaine d'oranges.
  5. Tu me rapportes un paquet de riz.
  6. Il me faut un morceau de gâteau.

C. (12 points: 2 points per item)
  1. N'oublie pas
  2. Pourquoi pas?
  3. Achète-moi; Bon, d'accord!
  4. Tu peux; je ne peux pas maintenant

Alternative Quiz 8-3A

A. (7 points: 1 point per item)
  1. g; **2.** c; **3.** b; **4.** a; **5.** d; **6.** f; **7.** e

B. (12 points: 2 points per item)
  1. a; **2.** b; **3.** c; **4.** b; **5.** a; **6.** b

C. (10 points: 2 points per item)
  1. Nous voulons des sandwiches au fromage.
  2. Je ne prends pas de gombos.
  3. Vous voulez de l'eau minérale.
  4. Tu veux de la viande.
  5. Ils prennent des fraises.

D. (6 points: 1 point per item)
  1. Non, nous n'en avons pas.
  2. Oui, nous en avons.
  3. Oui, nous en avons.
  4. Non, nous n'en avons pas.
  5. Oui, nous en avons.
  6. Non, nous n'en avons pas.

Answers to Alternative Quizzes 9-1A, 9-2A, and 9-3A

Alternative Quiz 9-1A

A. (8 points: 1 point per item)
1. as passé
2. sommes allées
3. ai vu
4. avez fait
5. avons nagé
6. avons mangé
7. ai pris
8. ai retrouvé

B. (10 points: 2 points per item)
1. a souvent vu
2. n'ai pas encore visité
3. avons déjà mangé
4. a beaucoup voyagé
5. a trop mangé

C. (12 points: 2 points per item)
1. Tu as oublié tes devoirs de géométrie?
2. Marc a rencontré un fille sympa au centre commercial.
3. Vous avez déjeuné tous les jours à la cantine.
4. Justine et Sophie ont retrouvé des amis au café.
5. J'ai travaillé au fast-food et j'ai gagné cent vingt euros.
6. Nous avons acheté quatre CD parce que nous avons trouvé cent euros.

D. (16 points: 2 points per item)
1. attendez
2. perds
3. vends
4. répondons
5. perdez
6. répond
7. vend
8. répondent

Alternative Quiz 9-2A

A. (7 points: 1 point per item)
1. b; **2.** c; **3.** f; **4.** d; **5.** e; **6.** a; **7.** g

B. (4 points: 1 point per item)
1. d; **2.** b; **3.** c; **4.** a

C. (8 points: 2 points per item)
1. ai perdu
2. a répondu
3. avez vendu
4. avons attendu

Alternative Quiz 9-3A

A. (10 points: 2 points per item)
1. h; **2.** d; **3.** f; **4.** b; **5.** e

B. (5 points: 1 point per item)
STUDENT
Qu'est-ce que je peux faire?
J'ai un petit problème.
CHERE MATHILDE
Pourquoi tu ne leur téléphones pas?
Ne t'en fais pas!
Tu devrais parler à tes parents.

C. (10 points: 2 points per item)
1. lui; **2.** les; **3.** la; **4.** la; **5.** leur

D. (10 points: 2 points per item)
1. b; **2.** c; **3.** a; **4.** a; **5.** b

Answers to Alternative Quizzes 10-1A, 10-2A, and 10-3A

Alternative Quiz 10-1A

A. (11 points: 1 point per item)
Pour l'hiver
un pull, des bottes,
un blouson, un cardigan,
un manteau, une écharpe,
un sweat-shirt
Pour l'été
une mini-jupe, un short,
un maillot de bain,
des sandales

B. (6 points: 1 point per item)
1. f; **2.** b; **3.** d; **4.** c; **5.** e; **6.** a

C. (4 points: 1 point per item)
1. a porté
2. ont mis
3. avons mis
4. avez porté

D. (14 points: 2 points per item)
1. Elle met une montre.
2. Tu ne mets pas de chaussettes.
3. Je mets un pull rouge.
4. Nous portons des bottes.
5. Elles mettent beaucoup de bracelets.
6. Thierry met une cravate.
7. Vous ne portez pas de ceintures.

Alternative Quiz 10-2A

A. (4 points: 1 point per item)
1. les bleues
2. les violets
3. la verte
4. le blanc

B. (6 points: 1 point per item)
1. maigrissez
2. choisit
3. grandissent
4. grossis
5. maigrissons
6. choisis

C. (20 points: 2 points per item)
Possible answers:
1. J'aimerais; pour aller avec; Je peux essayer
2. J'ai besoin de / Il me faut; en coton
3. Je regarde.
4. je cherche quelque chose pour; en coton
5. vous l'avez en 34?
6. C'est combien?

Alternative Quiz 10-3A

A. (5 points: 1 point per item)
1. la; **2.** les; **3.** l'; **4.** la; **5.** le

B. (10 points: 2 points per item)
1. démodée
2. petit
3. serrée
4. horrible
5. courte

C. (10 points: 2 points per item)
1. C'est / Il est
2. il est
3. Elle est
4. Elles sont
5. c'est

D. (10 points: 2 points per item)
1. Oui, je les mets en hiver.
2. Oui, je la prends.
3. Non, je ne le prends pas.
4. Oui, je les préfère.
5. Oui, je l'aime.

Answers to Alternative Quizzes 11-1A, 11-2A, and 11-3A

Alternative Quiz 11-1A

A. (12 points: 2 points per item)
1. Où est-ce que tu vas aller
2. j'ai envie d'
3. faire de la randonnée
4. Qu'est-ce que tu vas faire?
5. faire de la planche à voile
6. de la voile

B. (14 points: 1 point per item)
1. à; **2.** aux; **3.** à; **4.** au; **5.** au; **6.** au
7. au; **8.** en; **9.** en; **10.** à; **11.** en;
12. en; **13.** au; **14.** en

C. (8 points: 2 points per item)
1. Loïc et Stéphane vont aller chez leur grand-mère.
2. Tu vas aller en forêt.
3. Michelle va aller à la campagne.
4. Martin et moi, nous allons faire de la voile.

D. (6 points: 2 points per item)
1. aller à la montagne pour faire du ski
2. aller à la mer pour faire de la plongée
3. aller en colonie de vacances pour faire de l'équitation et jouer au volley

Alternative Quiz 11-2A

A. (5 points: 1 point per item)
1. Sors; **2.** Prenez; **3.** Pars; **4.** Faites;
5. Dors

B. (7 points: 1 point per item)
1. un cadeau
2. un passeport
3. un appareil-photo
4. un billet de train
5. une valise
6. un parapluie
7. un billet d'avion

C. (10 points: 2 points per item)
1. N'oublie pas
2. Tu n'as pas oublié
3. ne t'en fais pas
4. Bonnes vacances
5. Amuse-toi bien

D. (8 points: 1 point per item)
1. dort; **2.** dors; **3.** dort; **4.** partent
5. part; **6.** sort; **7.** sortons; **8.** sortent

Alternative Quiz 11-3A

A. (10 points: 2 points per item)
1. ai oublié
2. avons fait
3. a trouvé
4. avez parlé
5. ont pris

B. (5 points: 1 point per item)
1. e; **2.** a; **3.** d; **4.** b; **5.** c

C. (5 points: 1 point per item)
1. Oh, pas mauvais.
2. C'était ennuyeux.
3. Tu t'appelles comment?
4. C'était très chouette.
5. C'était épouvantable.

D. (10 points: 2 points per item)
1. C'était un véritable cauchemar!
2. C'était formidable!
3. C'était un véritable cauchemar!
4. C'était formidable!
5. Oh, pas mauvais.

Answers to Alternative Quizzes 12-1A, 12-2A, and 12-3A

Alternative Quiz 12-1A

A. (7 points: 1 point per item)
1. au; **2.** au; **3.** à la; **4.** à la
5. au; **6.** à la; **7.** au

B. (12 points: 2 points per item)
1. à l'épicerie; **2.** à la pharmacie
3. chez le disquaire; **4.** à la papeterie
5. à la pâtisserie; **6.** à la boulangerie

C. (12 points: 4 points per item)
Possible answers:
1. acheter des timbres; envoyer des lettres
2. retirer de l'argent; déposer de l'argent
3. emprunter des livres; rendre des livres

D. (4 points: 1 point per item)
1. regarde, voilà; **2.** là, tu vois,
3. Voici; **4.** là, c'est

Alternative Quiz 12-2A

A. (5 points: 1 point per item)
a. 5; **b.** 1; **c.** 2; **d.** 4; **e.** 3

B. (10 points: 2 points per item)
1. en avion
2. à vélo
3. à pied
4. en bateau
5. en voiture

C. (5 points: 1 point per item)
1. de l'; **2.** des; **3.** de; **4.** du; **5.** de la

D. (10 points: 1 point per item)
1. Hier, nous y avons rencontré Vincent.
2. Jérôme et Martin n'aiment pas y aller.
3. Marie-France y achète du beurre.
4. J'y suis allé pour déposer un chèque.
5. Tonio va y aller pour emprunter un livre.
6. Je vais y passer pour acheter du pain.
7. On y va très souvent.
8. Elles y ont acheté leurs livres hier.
9. Vous allez y acheter des timbres.
10. Tu n'y vas pas aujourd'hui?

Alternative Quiz 12-3A

A. (10 points: 2 points per item)
1. tu continues; **2.** tu tournes
3. Prends la rue
4. après traverse; **5.** Tu passes

B. (5 points: 1 point per item)
1. du; **2.** de la; **3.** du; **4.** du; **5.** des

C. (10 points: 2 points per item)
1. Pardon
2. Je cherche
3. s'il vous plaît
4. vous allez tout droit jusqu'au
5. C'est tout de suite à

D. (10 points: 2 points per item)
Possible answers:
1. entre
2. devant
3. loin
4. derrière
5. près